FOREWORD

"It's a privilege to own a business in Perthshire – an area rich and diverse in wonderful produce, producers and restaurants."

I had always dreamt of opening a restaurant in Scotland and after retraining at Leiths School of Food and Wine in London, I began to search for the perfect location to make this dream a reality. Alongside my business partners and co-owners Rachel and Andrew, we stumbled across Ballintaggart and everything fell into place. Started six years ago, we are a family business comprising a farm, cook school, exclusive use accommodation, wedding venue, shop and the nearby Grandtully Hotel, bar and restaurant.

I am immensely proud of what we have achieved as a business but also proud of the region that we work in and call home. We are surrounded by phenomenal scenery as we are rural but not too remote, meaning visitors and locals can access our venues easily and are spoilt by the varied nature of what our landscape offers us.

Our ethos is simple: to provide unforgettable guest experiences with an emphasis on Scottish seasonal produce and showcasing these ingredients in an uncomplicated way. Running our business in Highland Perthshire makes this job easy – we sit in a phenomenal culinary landscape and work alongside talented and passionate producers, many of whom are featured in this book.

Our menus at Ballintaggart feature Perthshire game and meat from local estates and farms, vegetables grown in our own kitchen garden and by other small local growers, Scottish fish and shellfish, coffee roasted in Perthshire, Scottish cheese and dairy products as well as foraged ingredients from our trees, fields and hedgerows. It's an honour to work with and showcase these ingredients on a daily basis and inspirational to be surrounded by such an amazing collection of producers, growers and restaurants who continue to raise the bar in Scottish food and drink.

When tasked with creating the Great Perthshire cookbook, I was keen to create a legacy that showcases some of the finest food and drink our region has to offer and I believe this book does just that. It has been a privilege to work on the book and I hope you enjoy it as much as we have enjoyed creating it.

BY CHRIS ROWLEY, EXECUTIVE CHEF AND OWNER, BALLINTAGGART

THE
PERTHSHIRE
COOKBOOK

WELCOME

This cookbook is brought to you with the support of Great Perthshire, the regional food and drink group for Perth and Kinross.

The role of Great Perthshire is to form a network of food and drink businesses that supports and promotes each other and showcases local produce. It has a strong tourism focus. The Great Perthshire network is committed to working with local business and partnership organisations to help grow the food tourism in the region. They want to be innovative and foster a culture of enterprise and knowledge exchange. In addition, they want to help the sector to inspire and encourage the next generation in their growth and development.

Food and drink is one of the largest industry sectors in Scotland and regional food is so important. Great Perthshire is looking to put local food and drink on the map and encourage people to be inspired by the outstanding produce Perthshire has to offer.

Chair of the group, Mark Bush, says: "The land and the climate are already here within the region and we are not short of passionate, creative people and businesses to make best use of the produce."

During September, Great Perthshire coordinates the Great Perthshire Food & Drink Festival, which showcases over 50 events and listings across the whole region. The festival allows everyone to take part, from producers and growers to chefs, mixologists and other talents. There's something for everyone. Past events have included tastings, pop-ups, afternoon teas, foraging trips, cocktail making, chocolate making, whisky and gin sampling: a bit of everything that makes Perthshire great.

Group coordinator, Sarah Russell, adds: "We aim to engage with our strong network of local businesses and encourage them to hold their own events under the umbrella of the wider festival. Perth and Kinross has a very strong food and drink presence, but in terms of tourism it also offers an exciting range of outdoor and heritage experiences for visitors and locals to explore and enjoy."

GREAT PERTHSHIRE X

FOREWORD

"I was all set to go to university to study acting but turned it down and decided to become a chef instead. I loved the energy and the rush of the kitchen."

My initial plans to study acting quickly changed after spending time in the kitchen at one of Glasgow's most popular restaurants, Stravaigin. I loved the kitchen's energy and rush, which led me to pursue my career as a chef.

Since then, I have had some incredible opportunities and experiences, from working with the team at Noma Denmark, Andrew Fairlie at Gleneagles and Hibiscus London, to becoming head chef at Bentley in Australia and Number One at The Balmoral in Edinburgh.

I am delighted to have been approached to contribute to The Perthshire Cookbook. It's an honour to feature alongside some of the finest chefs, producers and creatives in Perthshire, and being the first book I have contributed to, it is so special that this has been written about a place that means so much to me personally.

In 2021, I joined The Glenturret as executive head chef to build my team and open The Glenturret Lalique Restaurant, the first fine-dining restaurant within a Scottish whisky distillery. The distillery has a long-standing history and great heritage – as does Lalique – so it has been an exciting and rewarding role. In the restaurant, we have managed to create an innovative and engaging gastronomic experience inspired by the distillery, its environment and the genuine hospitality for which The Glenturret is renowned.

I am so proud that after just seven months of opening, Michelin acknowledged the hard work, creativity and dedication from my team and everyone at The Glenturret, awarding us one Michelin star. I look forward to what the future brings for the restaurant and my team.

Having the opportunity to live and work in Perthshire is genuinely fantastic. It is an area of exceptional natural beauty, and the abundance of fresh produce is second to none. We use as much local and Scottish produce as possible, including locally sourced Perthshire beef (Highland Wagyu), fish, shellfish, and fresh fruit and vegetables from Tomnah'a Community Garden. The team and I also enjoy taking the time out of the kitchen to forage in the woodlands just behind the distillery, where mushrooms, wild fruits, herbs, and flowers can be found.

Our Scottish heritage and surroundings are vital to the restaurant's heart and soul, and I hope that by sharing these recipes, you will be able to bring a small part of the essence of Perthshire into your home.

BY MARK DONALD

CONTENTS

ANYTHING BUT RUN OF THE MILL

The Aberfeldy Watermill Café and Bookshop is a quirky haven for browsing books and enjoying a hearty lunch and a cup of great coffee.

Established in 2005 by Kevin and Jayne Ramage amidst the curious setting of an old watermill, The Aberfeldy Watermill Café and Bookshop was initially focused on the bookshop, opened by none other than Michael Palin. However, the café became the obvious next step. Quickly becoming a thriving hub for the community, the café is best known for its predominantly plant-based menu of delicious lunches developed by chef Meg. Following lockdown, the Watermill was lucky enough to be able to welcome Morven to the kitchen, who shares the same love and passion as Meg for plant-based cooking, and the chemistry between the two is reflected in the creativity of the food.

The range of options is deliberately kept small and simple, ensuring that the food and drink remains top quality in the challenging environment of an original building that is not exactly spacious! Lovingly referred to as the 'Bat Cave', the kitchen can only fit two people in at a time but turns out nourishing soups, sandwiches and daily changing specials every lunchtime. Innovative dishes such as cauliflower 'KFC' wraps, stews and vegan pies draw on both the local Perthshire produce and inspiration from the travels of Meg and the team. All bread and cakes come from the award-winning Breadalbane Bakery and other local suppliers. Meat-eaters are also catered for by the excellent local butchers, MacDonalds, while Aberfeldy's zero waste shop, Handam, supplies vegetables, pulses and specialist vegan ingredients. Meg, Morven and the team have also begun working alongside Zero Waste Scotland, teaching people ways to make the best use of every ingredient.

Ambience is an important part of the Watermill's appeal. The dining area is full of nooks and crannies, allowing customers to find a cosy corner near the log burner or enjoy the outdoor seating. The unusual aesthetic is all part of the Watermill Café's charm, particularly the original mill machinery, which Kevin and Jayne kept during the refurbishment to showcase the building's history. The café's welcoming atmosphere offers bookshop customers, visitors and indeed locals a place to relax and enjoy a coffee or seasonal hot or cold drink made by the talented café baristas. The staff are well looked after by Kevin and Jayne, who are living wage employers and have maintained a happy family feel to the venture.

With both domestic and international accolades for the bookshop already under their belt, the possibility of a brand-new kitchen to expand on food options coming soon and plans for a Watermill Café cookbook underway, Aberfeldy's favourite café and bookshop is going from strength to strength as a well-loved hub of this close-knit village community.

THE WILD GARDEN BURGER

Preparation time: 25 minutes | Cooking time: 30 minutes | Serves 6

Creating our perfect burger recipe has been a labour of love; there has been a myriad of flavour combinations, plenty of mistakes and teamwork in our never-ending search for the ultimate vegan burger and now (though we may be biased) we think we've cracked it!

For the bramble ketchup

1 red onion, finely diced
2 sticks of celery, finely diced
1 red chilli, deseeded and diced
2 cloves of garlic, finely diced
2 tsp smoked paprika
1kg brambles, washed and drained
500ml apple cider vinegar
400g sugar
Salt and pepper

For the wild garden burger

1 red onion, finely chopped
3 cloves of garlic, finely chopped
180g chestnut mushrooms, finely chopped
Olive oil
2 tsp smoked paprika
1 tsp ground cumin
2 large beetroots, peeled
200g quinoa or brown rice, cooked
30g walnuts
30g gluten-free oats
90g sun-dried tomatoes
1 x 400g tin of black beans
2 tbsp tamari or soy sauce
6 bread rolls

Start by making the ketchup. Set the saucepan over a medium heat. Add the red onion and celery, cook until soft and translucent, then add the chilli, garlic and smoked paprika. Cook until softened and fragrant. Now add the brambles, apple cider vinegar and sugar. Leave on a medium heat so the sugar melts and the berries release their juice. Reduce to a low heat and leave to simmer while you make the burgers.

Preheat the oven to 190°c/170°c fan/Gas Mark 5. Place the red onion, garlic and mushrooms into the food processor. You may need to do this in batches depending on the size of your blender. Pulse until finely chopped.

Drizzle some oil into a non-stick frying pan and place over a medium heat. Cook the blended onion mixture with the smoked paprika and cumin for 10-15 minutes.

Meanwhile, grate the beetroot into a large bowl. Add the cooked quinoa or brown rice. Put the walnuts on a non-stick baking tray and toast in the oven for 3-4 minutes, or until they start to burn. Set aside to cool. Once the walnuts have cooled, place them in the blender with the oats and sun-dried tomatoes. Pulse until finely chopped. Add this mixture to the bowl of beetroot and quinoa.

Drain and rinse the black beans, add them to the bowl and mash with a fork until they are soft but still a bit chunky. Add the cooked onion mixture and tamari to the bowl. Season to taste with salt and pepper, then mix all the ingredients together with your hands. Shape the mix into patties.

Rinse your frying pan and set over a medium-high heat. Add a drizzle of oil. Sear the burgers on both sides for 4 minutes or until they are a lovely golden brown and starting to crisp. Drizzle some oil on a baking tray and transfer your burgers from the pan to the tray. Place in the oven for 20 minutes to finish cooking through.

By now your ketchup should be nice and thick. Turn off the heat and leave to cool. Once cooled, blend until smooth and season to taste with salt and pepper.

It is now time to assemble your creation. Add any toppings you like. We personally love this burger with a big dollop of pesto, a handful of rocket, a couple of parsnip crisps and a generous drizzle of bramble ketchup on top. Delicious!

FROM FAMILY FARM TO FOODIE PARADISE

Comprising rural accommodation, an events venue, The Cook School by Ballintaggart, plus a boutique hotel with restaurant, catering and a shop, Ballintaggart is a jam-packed destination for food lovers in Highland Perthshire.

Ballintaggart was established by family team Chris, Rachel and Andrew Rowley and the business began at Ballintaggart Farm in 2016 which remains at the heart of proceedings today. There you will find a special place to relax, restore and indulge. It offers refined rural accommodation with individually designed bedrooms, spectacular views in every season and a spacious kitchen for guests' use. It is also an atypical wedding and events venue, where long table dining is a speciality and menus showcase the best of Scotland's outstanding natural larder and, where possible, ingredients grown in the kitchen garden or foraged from surrounding fields and forests.

Ballintaggart Farm is also the home of The Cook School by Ballintaggart, where students can experience masterclasses which focus on sharing the expert knowledge and passion of our chefs – covering everything from fire and foraging to bread and pasta. Over the years, the business has grown and adapted and now includes the nearby Grandtully Hotel by Ballintaggart, an eight-bedroom hotel with a vibrant bar, The Tully, as well as an elegant restaurant, library and private dining room. The hotel was recently recognised with four stars by the AA and two rosettes for culinary excellence, thanks to the daily changing Market Menu in The Tully along with the seasonal set menu and tasting menu offered at the restaurant.

Also enhancing Ballintaggart's offer is The Feasts by Ballintaggart, a thriving catering and events team creating restaurant-quality dining from breakfasts and picnics to weddings and banquets alongside popular in-house products known as The Crop by Ballintaggart, which includes award-winning sourdough Sunshine Granola, jams and preserves. Finally, The Shop by Ballintaggart – online and instore at Grandtully and Aberfeldy – is the newest addition to the business. This provides a thriving base to stock up on Ballintaggart favourites, gifts and provisions including daily bakes, lunches to go, Great Taste recognised Ballintaggart Foraged Gin, The Tully Cocktails and their own Tully Table Beer.

However you discover Ballintaggart, Chris, Andrew and Rachel's team will ensure a relaxed and delicious experience, paying attention to the smallest details served with thoughtful charm. The ambition for the business remains the same: to grow and constantly improve, always striving to be a leader in Scottish and even global hospitality.

BEEF TARTARE, BALLINTAGGART GIN PICKLED ONION, SOY CURED EGG YOLK

Preparation time: 30 minutes | Cooking time: 10 minutes | Serves 4 as a generous starter or lunch dish

This has become established as one the signature dishes by Jordan Clark, head chef at The Grandtully Hotel by Ballintaggart. We use Ballintaggart Foraged Gin to pickle the onions, with the main botanicals – meadowsweet, nasturtium and lovage – all grown or foraged within a mile of Ballintaggart Farm.

For the beef tartare
400g frozen beef fillet
50ml soy sauce
50ml honey
25g chopped tarragon

For the pickled onions
4 banana shallots
100ml gin
100ml water
100g vinegar
100g sugar
2 sprigs of thyme
5 juniper berries

For the soy cured egg yolk
200ml soy sauce
4 egg yolks

For the sourdough croute
100g beef fat, melted
8 thin slices of sourdough

For the hazelnut crumb
150g hazelnuts

For the beef tartare
Finely dice the frozen beef into 0.5cm cubes and then allow to defrost naturally.

For the pickled onions
Finely slice the shallots. Bring the gin, water, vinegar and sugar to the boil, then add the thyme and juniper. Pour the pickling liquid over the shallots and allow to cool.

For the soy cured egg yolk
Place the soy sauce in a small bowl, carefully add the egg yolks and then cover with clingfilm. Leave to cure for 2 hours.

For the sourdough croutes
Drizzle the beef fat over the sliced sourdough and place in the oven at 180°c for 10 minutes until golden and crispy. If you don't have beef fat, you can use rapeseed oil instead.

For the hazelnut crumb
Toast the hazelnuts in a pan and then lightly chop.
To assemble the dish, mix the soy sauce, honey and tarragon together in a small bowl. Add the defrosted beef tartare and toss gently to coat, then divide evenly between the plates. Top each tartare with a cured egg yolk, two sourdough croutes, some pickled onions and hazelnut crumb.

BAKED SCALLOP

Preparation time: 45 minutes | Cooking time: 20 minutes | Serves 4

Showcasing Scottish seafood is a fundamental part of Ballintaggart and the team is passionate about featuring the very best of the West Coast's ocean larder on its menus. This is a simple but sensational way to enjoy scallops.

1 tbsp olive oil
1 red pepper, finely sliced
1 clove of garlic, crushed
1 red chilli, finely sliced
2cm ginger, finely grated
½ stick of lemongrass, crushed
1 tsp tomato purée
250ml good quality fish stock
100ml coconut milk
Handful of fresh coriander
4 hand-dived scallops
10g samphire
½ lime, zested
100g puff pastry
2 egg yolks, beaten
Seaweed or rock salt for serving

To prepare the Thai broth, heat a heavy-bottomed pan and add the oil. Gently cook the red pepper, garlic, chilli, ginger and lemongrass for 3-4 minutes. Add the tomato purée and continue to cook for 2-3 minutes, then add the fish stock and continue to cook until the mixture is reduced and has a syrupy consistency. Add the coconut milk, bring back to the boil and reduce again slightly. Season with salt and add the fresh coriander. Blend the broth in a food processor or using a hand blender, then pass through a sieve and allow to cool.

To prepare the scallops, slip a sharp knife between the shells and cut through the large white muscle tag to release one side of the shell. Pry open the shell and pull everything out. Using a spoon, neatly scoop out the meat. Separate the white meat from the outer skirt and roe. Rinse the scallops and keep them in the fridge on a paper towel. Rinse the shells and pat them dry.

To assemble the dish, cut the scallops in half through the middle and season with salt. Place 4 pieces into each shell and top with samphire and lime zest. Cover with 3 tablespoons of the Thai broth, then top with the other half of the shell.

Preheat the oven to 200°c. Roll out the puff pastry and cut into thin strips. Place a pastry strip around each scallop shell to seal the two halves together. Gently press the pastry in place to ensure that the seal is tight and there are no holes. Brush with egg yolk and cook in the hot oven for 10 minutes until the pastry is golden brown. Serve the baked scallops on a bed of rock salt or seaweed.

VENISON WELLINGTON

Preparation time: 6 hours | Cooking time: 1 hour | Serves 4

A Ballintaggart classic, originally made to bring cheer to tables at home in the depths of lockdown and now a well-loved dish prepared in our Aberfeldy kitchen by head chef Harris McNeill and his team. We use locally sourced Perthshire roe deer to add a wonderful wild flavour to our Wellingtons.

For the mushroom duxelles

500g flat field mushrooms

3 shallots, finely sliced

2 cloves of garlic, puréed

1 sprig of thyme, leaves picked

Rapeseed oil

Salt and pepper

For each venison Wellington

300g venison fillet per portion, trimmed

3 slices of prosciutto

2 tsp mustard

2 tbsp mushroom duxelles

1 square of puff pastry

2 egg yolks

1 tsp water

For the mushroom duxelles

Either finely chop or pulse the mushrooms in a food processor. Add a dash of rapeseed oil to a saucepan, place over a medium heat and add the shallots and garlic. Sweat down until lightly softened, then add the thyme and mushrooms. Cook on a low heat and season generously with salt and pepper to taste. Transfer the mixture to a blender and pulse, then transfer to a bowl, cover and chill until needed.

For each venison Wellington

To sear the venison, heat a frying pan over a high heat until smoking (without oil). Brush the fillet with oil and season well with salt and pepper. Place the fillet into the pan and sear each side for around 30 seconds until brown, including the ends. You will need tongs to help you do this. Place the seared fillet to one side until needed.

Overlap two pieces of cling film on a large chopping board. Lay the prosciutto slices on the cling film, slightly overlapping, in a double row to make a square big enough to encase the whole venison fillet. Spread the mustard on the prosciutto, followed by the duxelles, then sit the seared fillet on top. Use the cling film's edges to draw the prosciutto around the fillet, then roll it into a sausage shape, twisting the ends of cling film to tighten it as you go. Chill the wrapped fillet.

Unravel the fillet from the cling film and sit it in the centre of a strip of pastry. Beat the egg yolks and water together, then brush the pastry edges with this mixture, and the top and sides of the wrapped fillet. Carefully lift the pastry over the fillet, pressing well into the sides and sealing with egg yolk. Brush the outside of the pastry parcel with egg yolk to glaze.

At this stage, the Wellington can be frozen or placed in the fridge until needed. Before cooking, defrost thoroughly or bring to room temperature. Preheat the oven to 220°c or 180°c fan.

For medium rare, cook the venison Wellington for 18-20 minutes and then rest for 5 minutes. Serve with sautéed green vegetables.

CHOCOLATE AND BLACKTHORN SEA SALT CARAMEL TART

Preparation time: 2 hours | Cooking time: 40 minutes | Serves 12

A classic tart elevated with the careful skill of the team and the use of Blackthorn sea salt from the world's only working salt tower. This dessert is popular at both The Grandtully Hotel and The Feasts by Ballintaggart and is served with crème fraiche to provide a sharp contrast to the rich and decadent filling.

For the pastry
90g softened butter
65g caster sugar
3 egg yolks
200g plain flour
For the filling
200g softened butter
200g light muscovado sugar
1 tsp Blackthorn sea salt
200g double cream
200g dark chocolate chips
Crème fraiche, to serve

Preheat the oven to 180°c. To make the pastry, beat the butter and sugar together until pale and fluffy. Mix in the egg yolks one at a time, then stir in the flour until just combined to form a stiff paste. Tip the mixture onto a floured work surface and bring together to form a flat disc. Rest in the fridge for at least 30 minutes.

Roll out the pastry and use it to line the large tart shell. Rest again for 30 minutes in the fridge and then blind bake in the oven until the pastry is golden and the base is completely cooked through.

To make the filling, add the butter and sugar to a large saucepan and place over a medium heat. Simmer for 2 minutes before adding the salt and cream. Bring to the boil and simmer for 5 minutes, then remove from the heat and whisk in the chocolate until melted.

Pour the chocolate mixture into the baked tart case and leave in the fridge to set. Serve with crème fraiche.

A PERFECT MATCH

Barley Bree is a restaurant with rooms nestled in the village of Muthill between Gleneagles and Crieff, offering the perfect countryside retreat for breakfast, lunch, dinner and a cosy stay in Perthshire.

In 2007, Alison and Fabrice Bouteloup decided to combine their hospitality skills and knowledge by purchasing a former hotel close to the beautiful Perthshire Hills. They refurbished the old coaching inn, preserving some of the traditional rustic touches while freshening up the décor and reopening as a restaurant with rooms. With roaring open fires and outdoor seating, it's ready to welcome guests - no matter what the Scottish weather does! Named Barley Bree after an old Scottish phrase for whisky that appears in a Robert Burns poem, the establishment quickly became known for its delicious fresh food, thanks to chef Fabrice's classical French culinary background.

Barley Bree serves breakfast, lunch and dinner five days a week and showcases the best local produce across their short seasonal menus. A modern Scottish style combined with the classical French influences, plus flavours from around the world, ensures that there is always something new and interesting for guests to try. Certain signature dishes have emerged over time too, including the apple tarte tatin which is so well-loved by customers that it stays on the menu all year round. The restaurant's ethos is all about simple but really good food, using Scottish ingredients such as Strathearn cheeses, Stewart Tower Dairy ice cream, vegetables and salad from Tomnah'a Market Garden and the occasional Ardoch Hebridean sheep!

Having grown up around her parents' hospitality businesses and then worked in the wine trade, co-owner Alison is perfectly placed to complement her husband Fabrice's food with a carefully curated selection of wines and spirits, to be enjoyed in the restaurant or the hotel's small bar. She also credits restaurant manager Alma, sous chef Morven and housekeeper Vicky with Barley Bree's steadfast success and popularity. The close-knit team have scooped several awards over the years and, more importantly, built up a reputation for consistency and quality that's hard to beat. Known for their delicious food and friendly welcome, the restaurant with rooms is a firm favourite with locals and not to be missed by any visitor to this picturesque spot in rural Perthshire.

ROAST PERTHSHIRE GROUSE, POTATO RÖSTI & PICKLED BRAMBLES

Preparation time: 1 hour 30 minutes, plus pickling overnight | Cooking time: 1 hour | Serves 4

We use locally shot grouse in season from our local game dealer. The brambles and chanterelles are foraged from the countryside around Muthill and the baby leeks are locally grown, so this dish is a wonderful reflection of the beautiful Perthshire landscape.

50g water

50g caster sugar

50g red wine vinegar

100g brambles

2 large Maris Piper or King Edward potatoes

¼ tsp chopped fresh thyme

5 tbsp sunflower oil

150g unsalted butter

4 grouse (ask your butcher to remove the legs and back from the crown so you can cook them separately)

100g chanterelles

8 baby leeks, blanched

Salt and black pepper

For the sauce (optional)

1 shallot, chopped

1 clove of garlic, crushed

1 sprig of fresh thyme

1 bay leaf

35ml brandy

250ml demi-glaze (from your butcher or a good deli)

50ml double cream

Bring the water, sugar and vinegar to the boil, leave to cool and then add the brambles. These are best prepared in advance and left overnight in the pickling liquid.

To make the rosti, grate the potatoes into a bowl and add a pinch of salt. Leave for 10 minutes, then wrap in a cloth and squeeze out all the liquid. Return the potato to the bowl, add the thyme and season to taste with salt and pepper. Shape the mixture into 4 patties of 2cm thickness. In a frying pan, heat 1 tablespoon of the oil with 75g of the butter until foaming, then fry the potato patties on each side until golden brown.

To make the sauce, heat 1 tablespoon of the oil with 25g of the butter in a large pan. Fry the pieces of grouse back until caramelised, then add the shallot, garlic, thyme and bay leaf to cook until softened. Flambé with the brandy, reduce slightly, add the demi-glaze and reduce again. Sieve the sauce and set aside. When you are ready to serve, add the cream, season with salt and pepper to taste and warm the sauce through.

Generously season the outside and inner cavity of the grouse crowns and the legs with salt and pepper. Heat 1 tablespoon of the oil in a frying pan and cook the legs for 3 minutes, then transfer to a roasting tray. Heat another tablespoon of oil and 25g of the butter in a frying pan. Add the grouse crowns on their sides so that one breast is flat in the pan (cook in batches to avoid overcrowding). Once nicely coloured, turn the crowns over and repeat until all sides are golden. Transfer the crowns to the roasting tray with the legs and roast in a preheated oven at 180°c for around 5-7 minutes, or until the internal temperature reaches 55°c. The meat should be medium-rare as it will dry out if cooked for too long.

Meanwhile, heat the remaining butter and oil in a clean pan until foaming and gently fry the chanterelles for a few minutes, then add the blanched baby leeks and fry until tender. Rest the roasted grouse for 10 minutes while you reheat the rosti in the oven and finish the sauce, then carve the crowns to remove the breasts.

To serve, put one rosti on each plate, add the vegetables, place the grouse breast and leg on top and then scatter with the pickled brambles. Serve the sauce on the side.

CHOCOLATE TO GO WILD FOR

Charlotte Flower Chocolates is a small producer marrying the wild flavours of Perthshire with delicious fresh cream ganache and chocolate to make uniquely Scottish creations.

While working from home in a very rural location, keen forager Charlotte decided to try something completely new and explore the possibility of working with chocolate while developing her own small business. Charlotte Flower Chocolates began in her home kitchen, making friends and family happy with plenty of taste testing while gradually building up a customer base. Charlotte's experiment went from strength to strength, eventually converting a room in the house for production, and for the last ten years, chocolate-making has been Charlotte's full-time job. During that time, the craft chocolate sector also expanded dramatically alongside interest in foraging, inspiring and informing the burgeoning business as Charlotte herself gained more knowledge.

One of the challenges for Charlotte Flower Chocolates is to create wild flavours all year round, as spring and summer offer much more abundance than the colder months when foraging. From familiar flavours like elderflower, wild mint and hazelnut Charlotte has broadened her scope enormously, introducing mushrooms, seaweed, wild garlic, sneezewort and many more edible wild plants to her repertoire. Her signature chocolates are filled with fresh double cream ganache infused with seasonal flavours. Discovering more ways of incorporating flavour into the chocolate itself has enabled Charlotte Flower Chocolates to also offer bars and thins, truffles, chocolate-dipped treats and more.

Having set out to follow the seasons in chocolate, Charlotte offers a subscription scheme so customers can experience the whole range of wild flavours throughout year. She previously set herself the challenge of creating an Advent calendar of 24 wild flavoured chocolates, and even learned how to make chocolate from cocoa beans. The business is always evolving – one advantage of staying small – and isn't committed to large orders for retailers, so it can stay dynamic and follow Charlotte's own interests and passions. The handmade products are mainly sold directly to customers, though some small local independents do stock them such as The Chocolatarium in Edinburgh.

Alongside the online shop, farmers' markets in Perth and Aberfeldy and occasional food festivals, Charlotte Flower Chocolates also runs foraging walks so people can experience the beginnings of those wild flavours for themselves. Charlotte says that her rural location was a key factor in the establishment of her venture and is still a hugely important part of Charlotte Flower Chocolates: "All my wild produce grows within a short walk, or at most a drive away for coastal plants, so the flavours are incredibly fresh. It's pretty special to have such a beautiful and abundant landscape on my doorstep."

PINEAPPLE WEED ICE CREAM WITH THIN CHOCOLATE CRACKERS

Preparation time: 2 hours, plus freezing | Cooking time: 30 minutes | Serves 8

Pineapple weed (Matricaria discoides) is a common low-growing plant found on field and track margins, best gathered when the flower heads are new and the top two layers of leaflets are vibrant green. You can substitute this with any other aromatic herb or flower such as rose petals, mint or elderflowers.

For the ice cream

150-200ml pineapple weed

375ml double cream

125ml milk

2 egg yolks

100g sugar

For the chocolate crackers

15g butter

30g 100% chocolate (if using 70% chocolate, don't include icing sugar)

15g icing sugar

1 egg white

25g plain flour

Cocoa nibs or wild hazelnuts, chopped

For the ice cream

Use scissors to cut the top 2-3cm off each pineapple weed stem, then wash and pick it clean of any other plant material. Gently warm the milk, cream and pineapple weed in a saucepan, stirring all the time to prevent the cream burning on the base. Heat until the cream starts to steam, and before it gets to a rolling boil. Remove from the heat, cover and leave for an hour.

Reheat the cream, again stirring all the time, and then sieve out the weed. Whisk the egg yolks and sugar together in a heatproof bowl until light yellow, thick and the sugar has dissolved. Slowly add the warmed cream, whisking all the time, until fully incorporated.

Place the bowl over a pan of simmering water, stir continuously and heat gently until the temperature reaches 85°c. If you don't have a probe thermometer, the custard is ready once it coats the back of a spoon and leaves a trail when you run your finger through it. Plunge the bowl of custard into cold water. Once cool, cover and place in the fridge for at least an hour.

If using an ice cream machine, churn the custard until nicely frozen, then decant into a freezer container, seal and freeze overnight. If freezing by hand, pour into a freezer container to a depth of 4-5cm. Seal and place into the freezer for 1 hour 30 minutes, then remove and beat the ice cream to break up and distribute the ice crystals. Repeat this process at least twice until it is a thick and consistent texture. Level with the back of a spoon, seal the box and freeze overnight. This can be kept up to a month in the freezer but is best eaten fresh.

For the chocolate crackers

Preheat the oven to 180°c or 160°c fan and line a baking sheet with baking parchment. Put the butter and chocolate into a heatproof bowl and gently melt, stirring all the time. Remove from the heat and sift in the icing sugar. Stir until combined and then let the mixture cool to room temperature. Beat in the egg white and once mixed, beat in the plain flour and a pinch of salt.

Spread the mixture thinly onto the lined baking sheet, about 2-3mm thick. Sprinkle on the cocoa nibs or chopped nuts and bake for 15 minutes, until crisp. Remove, cool and break into shards. Store in an airtight container.

Remove the ice cream from the freezer 30 minutes before you want to serve it, then scoop into bowls and decorate with the chocolate shards.

DELIVINO HAS GONE WILD!

The newest (and wildest) addition to the Delivino family is a fully bespoke wood-fired outdoor kitchen, bringing outdoor dining to the people of Perthshire.

Delivino Wild Kitchen was born during the hospitality lockdown in 2020, starting as a simple idea that soon developed into a new approach to outdoor dining. What began as a 'portable pizza' concept soon became a bespoke, fully functioning outdoor kitchen offering the very best in wood-fired street food and sourdough pizza. The main attraction is a wood-fired oven capable of everything from slow roasting to intense searing, situated inside a custom-built shipping container which is fully moveable despite its huge size! With this set-up, the team can bring outdoor dining to their customers at anything from weddings and corporate events to festivals and pop-ups.

This unique dining experience offers an ever-changing menu based on the most amazing locally sourced and seasonal ingredients. Chef Director Stuart draws on these as inspiration for new creations and developing new flavour combinations. The Romana style sourdough pizzas are especially popular, focusing on quality over quantity when it comes to toppings, like San Marzano tomatoes and D.O.P balsamic vinegar from Modena. As for the broad range of street food, the philosophy is doing things a little differently so your typical burger or flatbread is elevated above the usual at Delivino Wild Kitchen.

Part of the successful Perthshire-based Delivino restaurant group, Wild Kitchen also functions as a testing ground for new ideas that can be developed into restaurant dishes. The first restaurant in Crieff was originally established as a wine bar and delicatessen in 2006, hence the name Delivino, then joined a few years later by the second restaurant in Auchterarder which shared the same concept and menu of relaxed and informal food and drink with Italian influences. One of the head chefs is a keen forager, providing the restaurants and Wild Kitchen with fresh wild ingredients, and this emphasis on local produce carries through to suppliers including their fishmonger in Perth and meat from Stuart's wife's family farm among others.

Stuart, who joined the business when Wild Kitchen opened, co-owns the outdoor dining venture along with Jamie and Frank who founded the first and second restaurants respectively. All three are hands-on when it comes to management, jumping into the kitchen on busy days where Stuart does most of the cooking. They are currently focusing on weddings and events that Wild Kitchen can cater for, but love to host pop-ups where they can introduce new menus. However, the longer term plan is to acquire a second trailer to expand Wild Kitchen's culinary capabilities, so watch this space!

CHILLI & FENNEL PORCHETTA

Preparation time: 1 hour, plus overnight | Cooking time: 4 hours 30 minutes | Serves 8

An adaptation of traditional porchetta using pork belly to create a delicious Italian inspired roast. Tip: change the flavours in the stuffing throughout the year to make use of the best seasonal ingredients available.

For the brine

2 litres water

150g table salt

150g light brown sugar

2 tbsp fennel seeds

For the porchetta

3kg boneless pork belly, skin-on

2 tbsp fennel seeds

1 tsp coriander seeds

1 tsp chilli flakes

8 cloves of garlic, peeled

4 sprigs of thyme, picked

2 oranges, zested

2 tbsp sea salt flakes

1 tbsp freshly ground black pepper

50ml + 2 tbsp white wine

2 carrots

2 fennel bulbs

2 white onions

2 fresh red chillies

4 cloves of garlic

2 tbsp olive oil

To make the brine, boil the ingredients in a saucepan until the salt and sugar have fully dissolved. Remove from the heat and allow to cool completely. Place the pork belly into a suitable container, cover with the brine and refrigerate for 24 hours.

Remove the pork belly from the brine and allow to dry, removing any excess moisture with a clean kitchen cloth. Place skin-side down on a chopping board and lightly score the flesh at 2cm intervals, then repeat at a 90° angle to create a diagonal pattern.

Heat the fennel seeds, coriander seeds and chilli flakes in a dry pan until they are lightly toasted and have released their fragrance. Tip the spices into a pestle and mortar or blender, add the peeled garlic cloves, thyme leaves, orange zest, sea salt, black pepper and the 50ml of white wine, then grind to a coarse paste.

Massage the seasoning paste into the scored flesh of the pork belly until fully covered. Roll the pork belly tightly and secure with butcher's string at 2-3cm intervals to ensure it remains tightly rolled while cooking. Place into the fridge to allow the skin to dry out as much as possible - this will help create perfect crackling.

Preheat the oven to 140°c and roughly dice the carrots, fennel bulbs, onions, chillies and garlic. Place the diced vegetables into a roasting tray and coat with the olive oil. Place the tray on a medium heat until the vegetables are softened and beginning to caramelise, then deglaze the roasting tray with the 2 tablespoons of white wine.

Place the rolled porchetta onto the bed of vegetables in the roasting tray and cook in the oven, uncovered, at 140°c for approximately 4 hours. After 4 hours, remove the tray from the oven and increase the temperature to 240°c (or the hottest setting). Transfer the porchetta to a clean baking tray, reserving the vegetables, and sprinkle the skin with sea salt flakes. Place the porchetta back into the oven for 20-30 minutes on full heat until the skin blisters, creating the perfect crackling. Once done, remove from the oven and allow to rest for 30 minutes.

To serve, carve thick slices of the porchetta and enjoy in a toasted brioche roll. Lightly mash the roasted vegetables to create a delicious condiment for spreading on your roll.

TOUR, TASTE AND EXPLORE

With deep roots in Perthshire alongside global brand recognition, Dewar's Aberfeldy Distillery offers the full experience when it comes to enjoying smooth Scottish whisky at its best.

Born outside Aberfeldy, John Dewar founded his shop in 1846 at 111 Perth High Street. His blended Scotch was made from other distillers' products according to his personal style: as smooth and fruity as possible. In 1896, his sons built the family's own distillery in Aberfeldy to supply the shop. Today, Aberfeldy Single Malt Whisky is still made in the very same building with craftsmanship and care. It is sold alone as well as an ingredient in Dewar's Blended Scotch. Their products are sold directly from the distillery onsite and online, as well as in independent whisky specialists around the UK and across the world.

Not only a working distillery, Dewar's is a hub for whisky lovers and novices alike thanks to the café, bar, production tours and tastings from a team that won at the Scottish Thistle Awards in 2018. All housed within the original building, the atmospheric café and bar repurposes the old malting floors with historical artefacts on the walls. During the day, the café serves delicious local food from Aberfeldy including soup and cakes from Dows, chocolate brownies by Ballintaggart, jam from Errichel and sandwiches from Piece.

At the bar you can go for a whisky flight to explore Dewar's extensive range of single malt and blended whiskies, or try a whisky cocktail which the team have developed to show that whisky can be fun and that sipping it neat in a leather armchair isn't the only way to enjoy Scotland's famous and sometimes mysterious tipple. To this end, they are also revitalising the tasting tours in 2022 to allow the guides to share their knowledge, demystify whisky and help everyone to appreciate the flavours.

Aberfeldy's signature style is characterised by citrus and honey flavours, which are created naturally during the production process as a result of the equipment and how it's used. The Aberfeldy 12 Year Old is the biggest seller, sitting alongside a flagship 21 Year Old and the annual release of a red wine finished whisky. They also own four other distilleries. Aberfeldy runs a program called Barrels and Bees which encourages bartenders to source high quality local honey and even keep hives on site where possible; Webster Honey have some apiaries in the hills above the distillery, showcased in both of their cocktail recipes featured in this book.

With a host of awards on the proverbial mantlepiece, Dewar's Aberfeldy Distillery is still passionate about producing the finest quality whisky and proud to be part of Perthshire's history and landscape.

· FINE SCOTCH WHISKY EMPORIUM ·

HOME of DEWARS

Dewar's Whisky

John Dewar & Sons Ltd.

ABERFELDY

The Dewar Highlander

Dewar's White Label

ABERFELDY HONEY HIGHBALL

Preparation time: 5 minutes | Serves 1

A highball is a refreshing long drink that works particularly well with a meal or on a warm day. Several newspaper articles credit one of our founders, Tommy Dewar, with creating it. This version highlights the key flavours of Aberfeldy Single Malt with more intensity than a traditional highball.

40ml Aberfeldy 12 Year Old
20ml local honey syrup*
Chilled camomile tea
Lemon twist, to garnish
Ice

Add all the ingredients to a chilled highball glass with cubed ice and stir. Serve without a straw.

ABERFELDY GOLD FASHIONED

Preparation time: 5 minutes | Serves 1

The Old Fashioned cocktail has taken the world by storm, but it can be tricky to find the right balance when using granulated sugar. This recipe uses honey syrup and orange bitters to accentuate our Aberfeldy single malt whisky, which has deposits of alluvial gold in its water source. There are plenty of small tweaks that will make this cocktail more personal, like different garnishes or types of honey.

50ml Aberfeldy 12 Year Old
10ml local honey syrup*
2 dashes Angostura Bitters
2 dashes orange bitters
Orange peel, to garnish
Ice

Add the ingredients to a mixing glass and stir for the desired dilution. Strain into a chilled rocks glass with a block of ice. Serve without a straw.

*To make your own honey syrup, combine equal parts hot water and local, high-quality honey in a glass. Stir until the honey is integrated and then allow to cool. This can be stored in the fridge until ready to use. Why not experiment with different types of honey?

LOCAL, SOCIAL AND GOOD!

From their café and professional kitchen in Perth, as well as creating tasty food and drinks, Giraffe gives opportunities to people from all over Perth and Kinross and beyond.

Giraffe Café offers the best local produce, carefully prepared by a team of professional chefs and trainees, in a calm and cosy space on South Street in Perth. Alongside the varied menu of delicious, freshly prepared food, Giraffe also offers professional outside catering for all occasions and home-cooked, nutritious and delicious meals that can be ordered or bought from the café. The social enterprise was founded to provide a supportive environment for work experience training, as there were not many businesses or environments set up to really help, support and understand those with learning disabilities, autism and mental health difficulties.

As a social enterprise, everything they do takes a 'community first' approach. This means that all money made from the various activities goes back into training or building on the future for trainees. The kitchen and café are the training site for those learning skills in the kitchen and front of house, as well as building confidence that will enrich lives and create opportunities for the future. Giraffe also runs other projects including Community Meals, which saw over 52,000 distributed locally to those in need between April 2021 and September 2022, and partners with other local charities and agencies each year to give over 1000 people a special Christmas meal too.

The café serves contemporary, tasty, honest food with a Scottish twist. Known for its hearty breakfasts and wide range of options to suit many dietary requirements, Giraffe is also committed to sourcing local produce and reducing food waste wherever possible. The team have a great relationship with nearby family-run Lindsay's the Butcher, and they often take donations from local farmers and use excess food from Fareshare when possible. Their incredibly popular themed supper clubs draw on staff and volunteers' love for food and community, showcasing cuisines and ingredients from Cajun to Scottish venison.

The whole team's dedication and enthusiasm is a huge part of what makes Giraffe tick. This includes Sarah Russell, who used to work in the South African wine industry; CEO Gareth Ruddock, an Irish ex-chef; and rosette-standard Scottish chef Steven Pearson. "We aim to foster a reassuring environment that allows everyone a chance at employment and inclusion," says Sarah, "and our superstar trainees really make the café a special place with a lovely atmosphere." They are now building a Community Kitchen that will allow meals to be scaled up in the future and provide more opportunities in hospitality and beyond.

GIRAFFE FISH PIE

Preparation time: 60-90 minutes | Cooking time: 45-60 minutes | Serves 6-8

A great warming dish that's easy to prepare and a firm family favourite. Why not add something a little different to mix it up: prawns, queenie scallops or a touch of curry powder perhaps?

For the mash topping

1.5kg Rooster or Maris Piper potatoes, peeled

200ml double cream

50ml milk

50g butter, melted

For the fish pie mix

3 eggs

60g butter

400g leek, diced (about 3 leeks)

1 Knorr vegetable stock pot

100ml double cream

140g smoked haddock

130g salmon

130g cod

80g garden peas

½ small bunch of chives, chopped

¼ tsp ground nutmeg

2 lemons, zested

75g cheddar cheese

Salt and pepper

For the mash topping

Preheat the oven to 200°c/180°c fan/Gas Mark 6. Prick each potato a few times with a knife (to prevent them from bursting) and bake on a baking tray for 1 hour to 1 hour 30 minutes, or until soft when pressed. Cut the potatoes in half and scoop out the flesh into a bowl, saving the skins for another day. Mash the potato with a fork or ricer and then while it is still hot, mix in the cream and milk to make a smooth mash. Season to taste with salt and pepper, then set aside.

For the fish pie mix

While the potatoes are baking, make the filling. First, put the eggs on to soft boil. Melt the butter in a small pot on a medium heat and cook the leeks slowly with the stock pot for 10 minutes until they are sweet and tender, then season to taste with salt and pepper. Now pour in the cream and simmer for about 10 minutes until reduced by half. Remove from the heat, blend with a stick blender, then set aside. Once the eggs are done, let them cool before peeling and roughly chopping.

Skin the fish and cut into bite-size pieces. Stir the haddock, salmon and cod into the creamy leek sauce along with the boiled egg, peas, chives, nutmeg and lemon zest. Transfer the mixture to a medium baking dish and then sprinkle with the grated cheddar.

Top the fish pie mix with the mashed potato, smoothing it over to cover the fish, then brush the mash with melted butter. Bake in the preheated oven for 25-30 minutes until the mash has turned golden brown, then serve with your favourite greens or salad.

GIRAFFE OATCAKES

Preparation time: 20-30 minutes | Cooking time: 12-15 minutes | Makes 80-100

One of our trainees' favourite items to make, these tasty oatcakes are a firm favourite in the café,
whether served with soup or a lovely terrine.

Chef's tip: this mix is best worked when still warm.

680g medium oatmeal
454g self-raising flour
43g caster sugar
1½ tsp salt
454g butter
3 tbsp water

Toast half the oatmeal in the oven until slightly browned, then combine all the dry ingredients in a large mixing bowl.

Melt the butter with the water in a microwave until liquid but not boiling, then pour in with the dry ingredients and stir until the dough comes together.

Roll out the dough on a lightly floured bench to a thickness of 2cm. Use an 8cm ring cutter to stamp out circles, rerolling until the dough is all used up.

Place the oatcakes on a baking tray and bake for 12-15 minutes at 180°c until golden. Allow to cool slightly before transferring them from the baking tray to a wire cooling rack.

Store in an airtight container once completely cooled.

COFFEE AND COMMUNITY

Glen Lyon Coffee have strived from the start to prove that the coffee community can work towards positive change. They pioneered compostable coffee packaging in Scotland, use solar to power their Aberfeldy roastery and plant trees in the Highlands to pay back their carbon debt.

Set up in 2011 in Perthshire's beautiful and remote Glen Lyon, founder Fiona Grant bought her first coffee roaster on eBay, installed it in the bothy next to her house and started selling small batch roasts at local farmers' markets. After a couple of winters digging coffee deliveries out of snow drifts on the glen's single track road, the roastery moved to nearby Aberfeldy on the banks of the River Tay. Now a team of eight, they have two state-of-the-art roasting machines, a community-focused roastery café and supply coffee wholesale to delis, cafés and restaurants throughout Scotland.

At the core of the business is a passion for delicious coffee and a commitment to ethically sourcing and roasting some of the world's finest beans. The Glen Lyon team travel regularly to origin to visit producers and build long-term, sustainable relationships. Coffee is sourced seasonally from Latin America and Africa, and they have direct trade links with farms in Bolivia, Brazil, Guatemala and Costa Rica.

A certified B Corp with a mission to put people and the environment before profit, Glen Lyon are committed to making their impact on the planet a positive one. Their packaging is fully compostable, they make local deliveries in the company's electric car and have invested in solar panels at their roastery. As well as planting trees every year to offset their carbon footprint, they have partnered with the Scottish rewilding charity 'Trees for Life' and a percentage of sales from True North, their latest blend, raise funds for the charity.

The Glen Lyon roastery lies at the heart of their Highland Perthshire community. As well as the busy Roastery Café which provides a hub for the community to meet and catch up, the roastery also hosts a monthly buzzing Repair Café dedicated to repairing and mending everything from toy cars to electronics and furniture for free. They've even been known to hold the occasional 'beer share' and barbecue as well as regular blues and folk nights. In 2021, Glen Lyon set up a Coffee Academy through their sister charity Project Northern Lights, which mentors young people in the community though a programme of barista skills qualifications and work placements. Their aim is to support young people in the area into work across Scotland and beyond.

BBQ BRISKET
BY HARRIS MCNEILL, HEAD CHEF AT THE FEASTS BY BALLINTAGGART

Preparation time: 24 hours | Cooking time: 10-14 hours, plus resting | Serves 8-10

There are many methods and differing strong opinions about how to achieve the best BBQ brisket.
I am not claiming that this is the best way, but this is our way, and we believe it creates something
wonderful with the fantastically rich Glen Lyon Coffee glaze.

100g Blackthorn salt

200g course ground pepper

200g ground Glen Lyon Coffee's Red Stag espresso

5kg point end brisket (ask your butcher to trim it)

2 bottles of quality red wine

1 litre beef stock

4 tbsp honey

500g Glen Lyon's signature Red Stag espresso beans

Cooking a whole brisket is a big undertaking and requires a lot of time and patience, so we recommend cooking a smaller section and asking your butcher for a trimmed point end. It's thicker and fattier so it can take more heat and is less likely to dry out.

Liberally sprinkle the salt, pepper and ground Red Stag espresso all over the brisket, making sure you get into all the nooks and crannies. Salt not only increases flavour but also helps to break down protein fibres which will give you a juicier bit of meat. Place on a tray and leave uncovered in the fridge for up to 24 hours.

At this stage we can go full American style and use a barbecue for around 12 hours of slow cooking. However, for home cooking, preheat your oven to 130°c and transfer the brisket to a tray large enough to contain it and all the liquid. Pour in the wine and stock, then cook for 6 hours, or until the internal temperature is around 90°c. Strain the liquid into a saucepan, then add the honey and the whole Glen Lyon coffee beans. Reduce this to a thick glaze.

Next, light your barbecue and wait until the coals are grey and there are no flames – you're aiming for a temperature of 130°c and maintaining this throughout will help the brisket to cook evenly. Place the brisket onto a smoking rack and brush generously with the honey glaze, leaving the coffee beans in, then place on the barbecue. Set a timer for 30 minutes and glaze again when it goes off, then repeat this process every half hour for 3 hours, making sure you reserve some glaze for serving. You can add more coals at each stage to maintain the correct heat.

Once done, wrap the barbecued brisket in baking parchment or butcher's paper, then again in tin foil, and place in an empty cool box to retain the heat. Resting the meat is just as important as cooking it, so leaving the brisket wrapped and sealed for 3-6 hours can really make a difference. The end result will be well worth the wait!

After resting, unwrap the brisket and heat the remaining glaze. Brush the brisket for one last time, then slice across the grain to help increase the tenderness. Serve with corn on the cob, broccoli and brioche rolls.

DINING, DISTILLED

The Glenturret set out to achieve something that had never been done before: to create a successful fine dining experience within a Scottish whisky distillery and redefine the concept of food, influenced by the traditional processes involved in whisky making.

Situated within Scotland's oldest working distillery, The Glenturret Lalique Restaurant was awarded its first Michelin Star within just seven months of opening its doors in July 2021. The restaurant was launched by The Glenturret Distillery in partnership with French crystal house Lalique, who have a history of supporting exceptional fine dining establishments. The eclectic and elegant multi-course tasting menu is playfully executed by an award-winning hospitality team – headed up by Scottish executive head chef Mark Donald and restaurant manager Emilio Munoz – and complemented by an extensive international wine list, curated by executive sommelier Julien Beltzung.

The menu changes with each season and includes clever nods to the distillery throughout. Temperatures used in the production process are mirrored in the cooking techniques to create several of the dishes and distillery by-products are included throughout the dining experience. This unique and innovative approach takes the form of vinegar aged in whisky casks and used as a dressing for fresh oysters, spent barley from the mash tun mixed into the bread dough and Peat Smoked 10 Years Old whisky chocolates for petit fours, to name a few.

Head chef Mark draws inspiration from his travels, applying new ideas and cooking techniques to the Scottish produce that features throughout the restaurant's menu. This includes locally sourced Perthshire beef and game, with a large portion of the fresh fruit and veg supplied by Tomnah'a Market Garden and supplemented by the team's own foraging expeditions around the distillery and River Turret. From Highland Wagyu to Lobster Toddy, each dish is a truly Scottish culinary experience, with one of the returning firm favourites being a reimagined version of a tattie scone.

Under previous ownership The Glenturret was chosen as the brand home of the Famous Grouse; however, it is now completely focused on its own whisky distilling and how that pairs and interacts with Lalique's gastronomic ambitions to surprise and delight diners. This new direction has been widely recognised with accolades for the restaurant as well as individual members of the team, including 4 AA Rosettes for Culinary Excellence, Scottish Pastry Chef of The Year 2021 for Kayleigh Turner and the Roux Scholarship of 2022 for Jonnie Ferguson.

HIGHLAND WAGYU GOOSE SKIRT WITH BEETROOT & PEAT SMOKED BONE MARROW

Preparation time: 20 minutes | Serves 4

This is part one of the overall recipe, which includes the Smoked Bone Marrow, Garlic and Salsify Mustard, and Blackcurrant Bitter Leaf.

For the bone marrow
1 litre sparkling water
70g salt
200g bone marrow

For the mustard
125g peeled & steamed salsify
90g hung yoghurt
85g good quality Dijon
75g confit garlic
30g fresh yuzu juice
0.3g xanthan gum
80g grapeseed oil

For the bitter leaf
1 head of round radicchio
200g blackcurrant vinegar
100g rice wine vinegar
50g mirin

For the bone marrow
Make a solution with the sparkling water and salt. Immerse the marrow in this solution and allow the salt and carbonated water to draw out the blood. Change the water if necessary. The bone marrow can be soaked this way in the fridge for up to 2 days prior to serving the dish, depending on the size of the marrow. Once blood-free, place the marrow on a tray and place that on a tray filled with ice to keep it cold.

For the mustard
In a blender, mix all ingredients except the oil to a very smooth paste. Using 30g of the grapeseed oil, emulsify the paste in the blender, then pass it through a chinois into a bowl set over another bowl of ice to cool the mixture down.

For the bitter leaf
Break the radicchio down into individual leaves, keeping the very outermost leaves for another use. Mix all the liquids together to create a vinaigrette. Place the radicchio in a metal bowl with the vinaigrette and cover with cling film several times. Leave to marinate.

HIGHLAND WAGYU GOOSE SKIRT WITH BEETROOT & PEAT SMOKED BONE MARROW

Preparation time: 1 hour | Cooking time: 1 hour | Serves 4

This is part two of the overall recipe, which includes the Cooked Beetroot and Beetroot Glaze as well as the smoking process for the bone marrow you prepared in the previous recipe.

Highland Peat, for smoking
4 medium-size crapaudine beetroots
4 sprigs of thyme
2 sprigs of rosemary
2 cloves of garlic, smashed
Cold-pressed rapeseed oil
500ml beetroot juice
Red wine vinegar, to taste

Light a small fire or barbecue with a lid or chamber attached. Once the coals are glowing and starting to die down, place some peat on top to start the smoking process. Put the marrow and ice set-up from the previous recipe over the smoke and close the lid. Smoke for approximately 1 hour, turning occasionally and making sure the marrow doesn't melt.

Wash and peel the beetroots, place them in a bowl and season liberally with salt. Add the thyme, rosemary and smashed garlic. Cook en papillote at 180°c with a decent glug of cold pressed rapeseed oil (we use a Highland one). The beetroot should take a minimum of 40 minutes and be caramelised and fully cooked. Check with a cake tester to make sure it's soft in the centre.

In a medium pot, reduce the beetroot juice, skimming when necessary. A thick glaze is what you are looking for. You should be left with about 100g of liquid. Season well with a nice red wine vinegar. The glaze should be thick and punchy.

HIGHLAND WAGYU GOOSE SKIRT WITH BEETROOT & PEAT SMOKED BONE MARROW

Preparation time: 1 hour | Cooking time: 30 minutes | Serves 4

This is part three of the overall recipe, which includes the Highland Wagyu Goose Skirt and Beef Sauce as well as the plating of the whole dish.

1kg Highland Wagyu goose skirt

Salt, pepper, oil

400g beef trim, diced

120g sliced shallot

100g sliced mushroom

75g Port

225g red wine you would drink

150g beetroot juice

600g veal stock

300g brown chicken stock

Pickled wild garlic vinegar

Beetroot powder

Toasted caraway seeds

Hairy bittercress

Trim the goose skirt, removing any inedible silver skin and sinew. Cooking from room temperature, season the skirt well with salt, pepper and oil before grilling over very hot coals. Turn the meat regularly and brush it with rendered smoked bone marrow fat from the scraps of the smoking process. Rest the beef once cooked to your liking.

In a medium pan, caramelise the beef trim, then remove and set aside. In the same pan, cook the shallot and mushroom until soft, then add the Port and reduce. Repeat with the red wine and then the beetroot juice, reducing the latter until syrupy. Add the beef trim back to the pan with the two stocks and bring to the boil. Once up to the boil, turn the heat down and cook slowly for a few hours until the beef has given all its flavour to the liquid. This can be done much faster in a pressure cooker if you have one. Pass and reduce to your taste. Season the sauce with pickled wild garlic vinegar to taste before serving.

To assemble the dish, take four plates and dust them lightly with beetroot powder. Glaze the cooked beetroot with the beetroot glaze. Sprinkle toasted caraway seeds on the glazed beets and put them on the plate pointing south-west. Dot a few small pieces of hairy bittercress over the glazed beetroot. Make a small rocher of the mustard emulsion and place it next to the beetroot. Slice the rested goose skirt and divide between the plates above the beetroot. Make a small and pretty bundle with the marinated radicchio to the side of the beef. Warm the smoked bone marrow and beef sauce in a pan together, then pour into the middle of the plates to finish.

THE GLENFIZZ

Preparation time: 5 minutes (plus 40 if making cordial) | Serves 1

This recipe was curated by the Lalique Restaurant Bar to celebrate the local herbs and botanicals foraged from around the distillery grounds. We use dandelion cordial that we made this summer, but it also works well with any other homemade cordial you might have.

For the cordial

1 litre water

300g sugar

5g salt

3g citric acid*

750g to 1kg dandelion

For the cocktail

40ml Glenturret Triple Wood

25ml dandelion cordial

15ml verjus (good lemon juice will also work well)

20-30ml soda

For the cordial

Add the water, sugar, salt and citric acid (*use lemon juice if you can't find this) to a large pot and bring to the boil for 2 minutes. Once everything has dissolved, add the dandelion leaves and boil for 1 minute. Remove from the heat, cover and leave to infuse for 6 hours. Strain the cordial through a muslin cloth and bottle. This can be stored in the fridge for up to 6 weeks.

For the cocktail

Add the Triple Wood, verjus and cordial to a highball glass filled with ice, stir to combine and top with soda. This is a great cocktail to enjoy as an aperitif or on a hot day!

THE GLENTURRET BOULEVARDIER

Preparation time: 5 minutes | Serves 1

The Boulevardier or Scotch Negroni is a great twist on the classic Italian Negroni, with additional depth and flavour from the malt whisky which you don't get from using gin.

Ice cubes and blocks

40ml Glenturret 10 Years Old Peat Smoked

20ml PX Sherry

15ml Campari Italian Bitters

15ml Valentian Rosso Vermouth

Orange peel, to garnish

Add all the ingredients to a glass mixing jug filled with ice. Stir with a long bar spoon or similar until the drink is cold and has reached the required dilution. For us, this is around 30–45 seconds. Pour over the ice block in a glass and garnish with orange peel to serve. This recipe is also great as a pre-made cocktail to store in your fridge.

Notes

We have used our Glenturret 10 Years Old Peat Smoked in this recipe, as you can really taste the vanilla notes, but it works equally well with our Triple Wood expressions. We have chosen Valentian Rosso Vermouth from the Scottish Borders; it has flavours of rhubarb, cinnamon and sweet and bitter orange, all of which work well with both the Triple Wood and 10 Years Old Peat Smoked.

WILD BY NATURE

Highland Boundary is a pioneering spirit and liqueur producer using natural wild flavours to restore biodiversity and reconnect people with the lost stories of Scotland's stunning landscapes.

The story of Highland Boundary's Scottish spirits began in 2008, when biologists Marian and Simon bought a farm with a plan to rewild the land and restore its biodiversity. In planting various native species to achieve this, they realised the farm could also become a resource to help other people understand what a healthy ecosystem looked and tasted like. The first Highland Boundary spirit was launched in 2018, the first birch-based drink to be produced in Scotland for some 300 years; and this flagship creation remains their best seller, winning a gold medal at the largest spirits competition in the world, closely followed by the double gold medal-winning Larch and Honeysuckle Spirit released in 2020.

The unique nature of Highland Boundary's venture into wild botanical spirits – which used to be made in the UK hundreds of years ago for their medicinal properties but had been long forgotten – makes Marian and Simon true innovators. They create, distil, bottle and label everything themselves with a small team including one of their sons, only using sustainably hand-harvested Scottish ingredients. The majority of these are grown on their own farm, which lies on the fault line that divides lowland from highland in Perthshire and gave the business its name. As biodiversity has always been the driving force, they adhere to strict regulations about how much can be foraged from any given species and everything is sourced within two miles of the distillery.

Their products, which include liqueurs as well as the award-winning signature spirits, are sold in specialist spirit shops, farm shops and delis as well as from farmers' markets across Scotland. Several fine dining restaurants have also caught on, including 63 Tay Street in Perth. Thanks to Marian's extensive experience as a research scientist, Highland Boundary can also create bespoke products and cocktails to suit individual occasions or clients, while the Wild Cocktail Bar takes both alcoholic and non-alcoholic drinks made with Highland Boundary products to events around the country. In 2022, Marian and her team even developed a cocktail to match the winning garden at Chelsea Flower Show, reflecting a belief that tasting the elements of a landscape is one of the most powerful ways we can reconnect to nature.

"What we love most about our products is that the flavours are completely new and different," says Marian. "People can't believe they're all Scottish botanicals and they are fascinated by how our spirits are so rooted in this landscape."

HIGHLAND COSMO

Preparation time: 5 minutes | Serves 1

This is our twist on a Cosmopolitan, with a stylish addition from the forests of Scotland. Our Larch and Honeysuckle Spirit was a Double Gold Medallist at the San Francisco World Spirits Competition, and it makes a wonderful Cosmo packed full of tantalising flavours.

50ml Larch and Honeysuckle Wild Scottish Spirit

50ml cranberry juice

25ml Cointreau or orange liqueur

25ml lemon juice

25ml elderflower syrup

Ice

3cm orange zest

In a cocktail shaker, combine the Larch and Honeysuckle Spirit, cranberry juice, Cointreau, lemon juice and elderflower syrup over ice. Shake vigorously and then strain into a martini glass. Hold the orange zest about 10cm above your Cosmo and very carefully wave it over a lit match or lighter flame. Bend the outer edge of the zest in towards the flame so that the orange oils are released, then drop the zest into your drink.

WILD SCOTTISH MOJITO

Preparation time: 5 minutes | Serves 1

We like to call this The MacJito, our modern Scottish whirl on one of the world's most popular cocktails. We swap the white rum for our award-winning super-fresh Birch and Elderflower Spirit, then we punch up the floral tones by using elderflower syrup instead of plain or mint syrup.

5-6 sprigs of fresh mint

3-4 wedges of lime

50ml Birch and Elderflower Wild Scottish Spirit

50ml lime juice

50ml elderflower syrup (you can use an elderflower cordial for this)

Crushed ice

Soda or sparkling water

Place the mint sprigs and lime wedges in a large glass, then pour over the Birch and Elderflower spirit, lime juice and syrup. Using a bar spoon, vigorously mix and muddle the ingredients to release the flavour of the mint. Add a generous quantity of crushed ice, stir well and then top up with soda or sparkling water. Give it a final stir for good luck and serve.

SWEET-TALKING WITH CHOCOLATE

Iain Burnett is a Master Chocolatier with a passion for excellence. He's received over
40 national and international awards including Best Truffle in the World - twice!
His uniquely hand-crafted Velvet Truffles® are made with an exceptional fresh cream
and rare island cocoa for Michelin-starred chefs, clients and customers worldwide.

Scotland's most awarded chocolatier, Iain Burnett, works from his specially designed Chocolate Kitchen by the River Tay in the village of Grandtully in Highland Perthshire. The unique flavours and world class texture of his Velvet Truffles are the result of both rare ingredients and the extreme level of craftsmanship. His goal was to create a luxuriously smooth and "naked" pure ganache, with no hard chocolate shell – but using only natural ingredients instead of artificial flavourings and preservatives. It took him over three years and 150 adjustments in methods and recipes to achieve the first Velvet Truffle, and each one takes two days to hand-crystallise.

Iain uses real fruit and honey from local apiaries and flavours change seasonally due to his use of non-blended cocoa and fresh cream. The rare São Tomé Island cocoa has exceptional fruity, aromatic and spicy characteristics, shifting with each harvest, and he combines this with an extraordinary sweet, grassy fresh cream from local Scottish cows. Only the purity of ingredients and extreme craftsmanship allows all the flavours to show through.

Iain trains his small, dedicated team of chocolatiers in-house to meticulously handcraft the luxurious textures and flavours of the Velvet Truffles which have received over 40 awards, including twice judged the Best Truffle in the World out of thousands of chocolates from 40 countries by chefs, sommeliers and food experts. As one of Europe's leading truffle specialists, his client list includes Claridges, Gordon Ramsay, Albert Roux, Gleneagles, Harvey Nichols, British Airways First Class, Michelin-starred chefs, Master Distillers, governments and royalty.

A visit to the Highland Chocolatier in Grandtully is a unique experience where guests can enjoy a guided Chocolate Tasting Flight and experience the world of artisan gourmet chocolate. The dedicated team in the Chocolate Lounge offers a menu of Velvet Truffles, Velvet Pralines, Dipped Candied Fruit, hot chocolates, fine teas, coffees and cakes which they bake fresh daily. Adding to this pure delight for the palate, visitors can learn about the historic journey of chocolate from tree to truffle and the differences between gourmet and mass-produced chocolate in the Chocolate Exhibition. The chocolate and gift shop is a hit with locals and tourists and has often been described as a cross between Aladdin's Cave and Alice in Wonderland!

Top-left, top-right, upper-middle-right and bottom-right pictures all courtesy of www.HighlandChocolatier.com

DARK CHOCOLATE BROWNIES

Preparation time: 15 minutes | Cooking time: 25 minutes | Makes 10

Your tastebuds won't believe that these rich brownies are gluten-free! Made with ground almonds and no flour, they are a far cry from the dry and crumbly gluten-free options out there. These are one of the most popular cakes on our Highland Chocolatier's Chocolate Lounge menu - and for good reason!

250g butter

350g 70% couverture (pure) dark chocolate chips, plus 50g for topping

350g caster sugar

1 heaping tsp cocoa powder

1 level tsp salt

5 small or medium eggs

150g ground almonds

Measure all your ingredients into separate bowls. Preheat a fan oven to 170°c and line a deep 20 by 30cm tin with baking paper.

Melt the butter and chocolate gently either with 10 second bursts in the microwave or by warming them in a metal bowl floating in a large plastic bowl of hot water. Stir frequently until the majority has melted.

Now turn on the electric mixer at medium speed and add the ingredients one by one for the following amount of time:

Melted chocolate and butter: 30 seconds

Sugar: 3 minutes

Cocoa powder and salt: 30 seconds

Eggs: 30 seconds

Ground almonds: 1 minute

Pour the batter into the prepared tin and sprinkle the extra 50g of chocolate chips on top. Bake in the preheated oven for 25 minutes.

To serve

Cut the cooled brownies into 10 pieces and sprinkle some icing sugar on top. Serve alone or with whipped cream and fruit of your choice on the side. They go beautifully with a cup of your favourite coffee!

FROM FIELD TO FORK

Loch Leven's Larder was founded by Emma and Rob Niven in 2005 after they moved to the area and recognised an unmissable opportunity to champion local produce.

Nestled in a beautiful setting right on the Loch Leven Heritage Trail and close to the historic town of Kinross, Loch Leven's Larder is the perfect spot for a day out, whether you want to eat, drink, shop or explore the great outdoors. There are two cafés to choose from and a food hall brimming with fresh, local and homemade produce alongside an extensive gift shop specialising in European and design-led Scottish gifts and toiletries. Over a decade since its opening, the field-to-fork concept remains at the Larder's core while it has grown in many ways with great support from loyal, local customers as well as visitors.

Loch Leven's Larder is situated at the heart of the family-run Channel Farm and as such is passionate about traceability, provenance and seasonality. Emma, Rob and brother Mike are the third generation to farm the land, which stretches over 1000 acres. The Larder uses as much local produce as possible, from vegetables grown in their own fields to produce from the many artisan makers in the surrounding area and the rest of Scotland. The café menu changes with the seasons to showcase this approach; head chef Brian likes to use influences from other continents alongside home-grown vegetables, creating dishes such as Channel Farm carrot houmous. Other favourites include Pete's Buttie – named after Emma's dad and comprising locally sourced black pudding, prime Ayrshire bacon and free-range eggs from the East Neuk – and the daube of Highland venison with toasted sourdough. Homemade sausage rolls, bread and croissants from the on-site bakery always go down a treat, too.

The Greenhouse Café provides friendly, speedy service for those active customers who are walking, cycling or running in the area, while the Larder Café serves breakfast, lunch, hot drinks and cakes for more leisurely visits. The diverse options are family-friendly and make sure everyone is welcome all year round. Loch Leven's Larder is proud to have a great team, which has enabled the business to expand and become one of the area's biggest employers with over 85 staff. They've also scooped numerous awards including Scottish Thistle's 'Best Café and 'Warmest Welcome' alongside many that demonstrate the venture's success in retail, hospitality and business.

Emma is currently developing a Sensory Garden at the Larder, creating a space to relax and reflect for both customers and staff. Meanwhile, The Mustard Shed – a new home interiors and garden shop – will open in early 2023: yet another great reason to visit!

DAUBE OF HIGHLAND VENISON

Preparation time: 15-20 minutes, plus 24 hours marinating | Cooking time: 3-3.5 hours | Serves 4-6

Daube is a traditional French stew cooked slowly in a braising pan called a daubière, placed in an oven until beautifully tender. I like to use roe deer from the Highlands as it's very lean and has a rich flavour which lends itself perfectly to a classic daube.

1.5kg diced haunch of venison
1 bottle of red wine
250ml Port
4 carrots, cut into 1cm rounds
2 sticks of celery, cut into 1cm slices
2 onions, finely sliced
1 garlic bulb, cut in half
2 tbsp Herbes de Provence
5 tbsp olive oil
250g dry cured bacon lardons
2 tbsp tomato purée
2 tbsp flour
1 tbsp orange zest
600ml beef or venison stock

Marinate the diced venison in the red wine and Port with the vegetables, garlic and herbs in an airtight container in the fridge for 24 hours.

The next day, drain the meat and vegetables, reserving the marinating liquid, then pat them dry. Discard the garlic and heat a heavy-based lidded pan. Once hot, add the olive oil and fry off the venison and vegetables until golden brown. You may need to do this in batches. Remove from the pan once done.

In the same pan, fry the bacon lardons until golden, then stir in the tomato purée and flour. Cook for 1 minute, then pour in the reserved marinating liquid to deglaze the pan, stirring well.

Once deglazed, add the venison and vegetables back to the pan along with the orange zest. Reduce the liquid by half and then add the stock. Bring to the boil, then take the pan off the heat and seal in all the moisture by putting a 3cm strip of tin foil around the pan where the lid meets the base, making it as tight as you can.

Cook the daube in the oven at 180°c for 2 hours 30 minutes to 3 hours, until the venison is beautifully tender. Serve with Camargue rice for an authentic daube or alternatively with thick slices of warm bread.

A FOOD LOVER'S RURAL RETREAT

To relax, unwind and escape is the order of the day at this boutique hotel and restaurant surrounded by some of Scotland's finest scenery.

The Moor of Rannoch was built in 1890 to provide accommodation for the engineers constructing the West Highland Railway Line, and it has offered shelter to visitors exploring Rannoch Moor ever since. This vast wilderness covers some 120km² and features some of Scotland's finest scenery. Owners Scott and Steph aim to complement these surroundings in both the rooms and the restaurant, offering stunning views across the landscape and as much local produce as possible. With comfy lounges, log burners and a deliberate lack of TVs, radio and WiFi, The Moor of Rannoch is the perfect place to escape the constant connectivity of the modern world.

If the stunning natural setting doesn't tempt you – including red deer wandering on the lawn and eagles often spotted in the vicinity – then the food surely will. Proudly holding 2 AA Rosettes, The Moor of Rannoch's restaurant offers an intimate dining experience with a real focus on seasonal Scottish produce. Scott and Steph have developed longstanding relationships with local suppliers, including duck and quail egg farmers in Rannoch, Glen Lyon Coffee Roasters, MacDonald Butchers in Pitlochry and the nearby estate who provide venison. The owners themselves spend their days off foraging for spruce tips, wood sorrel, bog myrtle, mushrooms and much more, while growing their own herbs, leafy vegetables, berries and flowers in the kitchen garden to provide the restaurant with the freshest possible produce.

Steph creates a new menu each evening, ensuring that the kitchen can make the best use of all this fantastic local produce when it is in prime condition. The remote location means that they often depend on courier companies for deliveries and sometimes even in Rannoch parcels are delayed, so it's important to have a flexible approach to suit their surroundings. Scott and Steph are always on the lookout for new companies to partner with that can help develop their offering and recently started stocking beer from Wasted Degrees in Blair Athol. Their passion for great food and drink has taken them from jobs in hospitality to an 18-month adventure around the world, culminating in their purchase of The Moor of Rannoch in 2013.

With just five rooms and a restaurant that seats up to 18, the focus is firmly on quality over quantity. This has been justly rewarded over the years with accolades from Visit Scotland, Scottish Rural Awards and the Good Hotel Guide among others, proving that The Moor of Rannoch more than lives up to the splendour of its Perthshire setting.

ARBROATH SMOKIE AND FINE HERB TART

Preparation time: 1 hour | Cooking time: 1 hour 35 minutes | Serves 12

Arbroath Smokies add a wonderful flavour to this tart. It could be served either as a centrepiece for lunch, a picnic or as a starter for a dinner party. Don't throw out the fish bones and skin; they make a wonderful stock for soups and sauces.

For the pastry

250g plain flour

5g caster sugar

½ tsp salt

1 tbsp thyme leaves, finely chopped

150g unsalted butter, cubed

1 whole egg, beaten

1 tsp cold water

1 egg yolk

For the filling

4 Arbroath Smokies, at room temperature

430ml double cream

3 whole eggs

2 egg yolks

1 tbsp flat leaf parsley, finely chopped

1 tbsp tarragon, finely chopped

1 tbsp chives, finely chopped

1 tbsp chervil, finely chopped

1 lemon, zested

½ tsp sea salt

Black pepper

Preheat the oven to 180°c or 160°c fan. Place a baking sheet on the middle shelf. Combine the flour, caster sugar, salt, thyme and cubed butter in a bowl. Rub the butter into the dry ingredients between your fingertips until the mixture resembles breadcrumbs. Add the beaten egg and water, combine to form a dough, then wrap in clingfilm and rest in the fridge for 30 minutes.

Roll out the pastry on a lightly floured surface to 3mm thick. Line a 23cm fluted loose-bottomed tart tin with the pastry, ensuring it reaches fully into the corners. Trim away any excess, leaving the pastry slightly overhanging the edges, and prick the base with a fork.

Line the pastry with a triple layer of cling film, folding it over the sides. Fill the pastry case with uncooked rice or baking beans. Place in the freezer for 5 minutes, then place the pastry case on the hot baking sheet in the oven and bake for 20 minutes.

Meanwhile, lay each Arbroath Smokie upside down with the fins on a board. Open the cavity and gently press on the skeletal bones to release them from the flesh. The skeleton should easily pull away. Tease the flakes away from the skin, being careful to remove any small bones.

Take the pastry case out the oven, remove the rice or baking beans and clingfilm, then put the pastry case back in the oven for a further 10 minutes, or until golden brown. Using a pastry brush, paint the base and sides of the pastry case with the egg yolk, then place back in the oven for 3 minutes until the egg yolk is cooked. This creates a seal for the wet filling and stops the pastry going soggy. Now leave the pastry case to cool slightly and reduce the oven temperature to 160°c or 140°c fan.

In a jug, beat the double cream, whole eggs and egg yolks with a fork until well combined. Add the chopped herbs, lemon zest, salt and black pepper to taste, then mix until well combined. Evenly distribute the Arbroath Smokie flakes in the pastry case. Pour over the egg and cream mixture until the pastry case is full. Carefully place the tart back in the oven.

Bake the tart for 1 hour, then cool for 10 minutes before using a small knife trim off the overhanging pastry. Serve warm.

PEAR, BLACKBERRY & HAZELNUT CHOUX BUNS

Preparation time: 2 hours 30 minutes | Cooking time: 25 minutes | Makes 24

This is a dessert in three parts: choux buns, crème diplomat and caramelised pears. They can all be made in advance and, once plated, make for an impressive end to a dinner. The pears and blackberries can be easily substituted for any other seasonal fruit.

For the crème diplomat

500ml whole milk

120g caster sugar

1 vanilla pod

6 egg yolks

45g cornflour

250ml double cream, semi-whipped

For the caramelised pears

6 William Pears, peeled, cored and quartered

20g butter

60g caster sugar

50ml lemon juice

50ml Xante Pear Liqueur

For the craquelin

85g butter, softened

100g soft light brown sugar

100g plain flour

For the choux buns

225g cold water

100g unsalted butter

5g each of salt and sugar

180g plain flour, sieved

260g whole eggs, beaten

250g blackberries, halved

100g hazelnuts, toasted, crushed

For the crème diplomat

In a saucepan, warm the milk with 60g of the sugar and the vanilla pod. Whisk the egg yolks, remaining sugar and cornflour together in a bowl. Once the milk starts to steam, pour it over the egg mixture and whisk to combine. Pour back into the saucepan and continue whisking on a medium heat until the custard thickens. Pour into a bowl to cool, cover with clingfilm and chill in the fridge.

Whisk the custard to loosen and then fold through the whipped cream. Chill until required.

For the caramelised pears

Cook the pears in a dry frying pan on a medium heat for 10 minutes, stirring occasionally until they start to colour, then remove. Melt the butter in the same pan, then add the sugar and pears. Stir until tender, add the lemon juice and liqueur, then reduce for 5 minutes until the pears are coated in a glossy syrup.

For the craquelin

Cream the butter and brown sugar in a stand mixer, add the flour and beat until combined. Roll out the mixture between two sheets of baking parchment to 3mm thick. Store in the freezer to firm up.

For the choux buns

Place a deep tray in the bottom of the oven and preheat to 200°c or 190°c fan. Line two baking sheets with parchment paper.

In a medium saucepan, bring the water, butter, salt and sugar to the boil. Add the flour and stir to form a dough. Cook on a medium heat, stirring constantly until a crust appears on the base of the saucepan. Transfer the dough to a stand mixer with a paddle attachment and beat on a low speed for 3 minutes or until the steam has disappeared. Slowly add the beaten eggs, increase to a medium speed and beat until the mixture is glossy.

Put the mixture into a piping bag with a plain nozzle. Pipe 12 walnut-sized balls of choux onto each baking sheet, allowing plenty of space between them. Cut out 5cm discs of craquelin and place one on top of each choux bun. Place the baking sheets in the oven, carefully pour 100ml hot water into the deep tray to create steam and quickly shut the door. Bake for 25 minutes or until puffed up and golden brown. Allow to cool and then slice the top quarter off each choux bun. Fill them with the crème diplomat, caramelised pear, blackberries, and hazelnuts. Replace the tops and serve.

MURRAYSHALL HAS IT ALL

Whether for great food, adventure, chill seeking or exploring, Murrayshall has it all.

Murrayshall Country Estate is a luxury boutique hotel set in 365 acres of Perthshire countryside. Dating back over 400 years, it was the former home of Lord Lynedoch and has since been transformed into a magnificent Scottish hotel with 40 guest bedrooms and suites. Murrayshall also boasts two restaurants, a bar and 27-holes of parkland golf. The original brasserie has become Eòlas, a fine dining restaurant with its own identity within the hotel.

The country estate's mission is simple: to offer the best modern Scottish cooking, specialising in quality, seasonal food and local producers. The team want the diners to enjoy the dishes, create great memories and appreciate the value of good cooking techniques. Menus change every six weeks, strongly promoting the larder of Perthshire and beyond, using Scottish produce with quality ingredients and a focus on seasonal cooking. The hotel works with local suppliers as much as possible, including George Campbell fishmonger in Perth and John Henderson Meats in Glenrothes.

Head chef Craig Jackson has also introduced a five-course tasting menu alongside the fine dining menu in the restaurant, with a choice of wine flights. The team are well versed in the knowledge required to inform guests of the wines which pair each course. After receiving two AA Rosettes for Eòlas, Craig and his team are now striving for a third within the next 12 months.

Service is a top priority at the hotel and the aim is for guests to enjoy their time, feel looked after and benefit from informative but not intrusive service. Murrayshall recently won the UK's Best Boutique Hotel Restaurant with Boutique Hotelier Magazine and are up for several other awards including Visit Scotland's Regional Thistle Awards for Best Hotel and Luxury Lifestyle Magazine's Best Hotel for Food.

"We are excited by the progress that we have made in the last 20 months, but we have huge ambitions going forward to become a world-class lifestyle and leisure destination, which will cement us within Scotland's top flight of hotels."

Murrayshall plans to continue investing in the customer experience, and the next step is the addition of a beautiful spa which will include a swimming pool, spa pool, 18 treatment rooms and gymnasium. All this will be housed in a stunning building with floor-to-ceiling glass windows, making the most of the countryside views and enhancing the appeal of this tranquil place to stay and dine.

SCOTCH LAMB RACK AND NECK WITH ANCHOVY AND CAPERS

Preparation time: 24 hours | Cooking time: 6-7 hours | Serves 4

This dish was created by sous chef Paul Palombo and his tips for this dish are to have your butcher French
trim the lamb rack and tie string between each bone, scoring the fat for easier rendering, and to blanch
your vegetables in advance so they only need reheating, giving you more time to focus on the lamb.

1 lamb rack, 8 bones, French trimmed
1 lamb neck, boned and rolled
1 litre lamb stock
1 bay leaf
1 sprig of rosemary
50g flour, seasoned
4 eggs, beaten
200g breadcrumbs

For the salsa verde lamb rack
1 bunch of fresh parsley
1 bunch of fresh tarragon
1 bunch of fresh mint
1 bunch of fresh basil
1 tsp Dijon mustard
2 tbsp capers
2 cloves of garlic
12 anchovy fillets
200ml good olive oil
1 lemon, zested and juiced

To serve
Seasonal vegetables of your choice
100ml tarragon vinegar
12 black olives
2 little gem lettuces

For the lamb neck

Start this the day before you want to serve the dish. Preheat the oven to 150°c and brown off the
lamb neck in a casserole dish. Once the meat is sealed, add the stock, bay leaf, rosemary and 2 litres
of water. Cover and cook in the oven for 6-7 hours until tender, or use a slow cooker if you have one.
Once the lamb is cooked, strain the stock through a fine sieve and reserve for later. Place a small plate
over the lamb and weigh down with something heavy, then cover and chill overnight.
The next day, cut the chilled lamb neck into 12 evenly sized pieces. Dust them with the seasoned
flour, coat in the beaten egg and then the breadcrumbs. Chill until needed.
To make the lamb jus, simply reduce the strained cooking liquor from the lamb to a sauce consistency.
Keep warm until ready to serve.

For the salsa verde lamb rack

Put all the ingredients except the lamb into a food processor, starting with half the olive oil, and
blend to a paste, adding more oil if needed.
Rub half the salsa verde all over the lamb – only covering the meat, not the fat – and then leave to
marinate for 20-30 minutes. Preheat the oven to 160°c.
Place the marinated lamb rack fat side down in a pan to render gently on a medium heat for 8-10
minutes, then turn up the heat and brown the lamb all over. Transfer the rack to the preheated oven
and cook for 15 minutes. Remove and rest for 10 minutes in a warm place.

To serve

Cook the seasonal vegetables until tender, then remove from the heat and drizzle with some olive oil
and tarragon vinegar. Deep fry the breadcrumbed lamb neck until golden and crispy, then season
with salt to taste.
Spoon some of the remaining salsa verde onto the centre of the plate and place 3 pieces of lamb neck
around the salsa. Loosely arrange the vegetables in a ring around the edge, then divide the olives
and gem lettuce between the plates. Carve the lamb rack into 4 portions and place on top of the salsa
verde. Spoon over small amount of the lamb jus, then serve the rest alongside.

A LOCAL LOVE AFFAIR

The North Port celebrates Scottish produce by refining the flavours derived from its landscape and serving them in a friendly, casual, welcoming restaurant overlooking the River Tay.

The North Port is a restaurant created and run by chef Andrew Moss and his wife Karen, who manages front of house, to showcase the carefully selected ingredients they source from local growers, breeders, suppliers and foragers. They opened in 2014 after having searched high and low in Scotland for the perfect venue and location, which they discovered in Perth at the beautiful old building now housing their first venture. "It's a pretty unique space," says Andrew, "and still a work in progress as we are always aiming to improve our food and the restaurant in general."

Running their own restaurant has given Andrew and Karen the creative freedom they wanted, resulting in dishes that present "the best ingredients in the world" – mostly sourced from Perthshire, famed for its fantastic produce and passionately advocated for by Andrew – in a way that makes the most of their flavours without over-complicating them. The emphasis on local meat, game, dairy and vegetables even extends to foraging, done by Andrew and the team down the banks of the River Tay which is right on their doorstep. This ethos doesn't stop with food either: Scottish beers populate the bar, and there's even a selection of artisanal mead which is created nearby using natural botanicals.

The North Port's beautifully presented, refined and inventive food has already earned it two AA Rosettes, but for Andrew and Karen, ensuring guests enjoy what they do is more important than any accolades. The restaurant's welcoming atmosphere contributes to this goal, enhanced by features such as wood panelling which keeps the dining rooms cosy during the evening and bright during the day. Tables are well spaced to offer guests an intimate experience, which reflects the precision and care taken with flavours on the plate. Friendly, relaxed service sets the scene for a casual meal out, while special occasion dining in the private Tay Room can be tailored to any tastes. "Everyone working here gets what we're about in terms of both food and service," says Andrew, "so we share a commitment to the guests that runs through everything we do."

PIGEON, BEETROOT, BRAMBLES

Preparation time: 24 hours | Cooking time: 3-6 hours | Serves 4 as a starter

This autumnal dish makes great use of some lovely Scottish ingredients, contrasting the gamey flavour of pigeon with the earthy beetroot and sweet yet sharp brambles. The perfect dinner party dish: nearly everything can be done in advance and the vibrant colours are sure to impress.

4 pigeon breasts

6 brambles, halved

25g blanched & toasted hazelnuts, crushed

For the cooked beetroot

2 each golden and purple beetroot

100ml cold pressed rapeseed oil

2 sprigs of thyme & 10g salt

For the pickled beetroot

100ml each cider vinegar & white wine

100g sugar, 5g salt & 2 bay leaves

1 tsp each coriander seeds, fennel seeds and black peppercorns

1 small golden beetroot

For the bramble ketchup

4 banana shallots, diced

50g ginger, peeled and diced

2 cloves of garlic, crushed

1 tsp each coriander seeds, fennel seeds and mustard seeds

250g brambles

125ml cider vinegar & 100g caster sugar

For the hazelnut mayo

250g blanched and toasted hazelnuts

2 egg yolks & 2 tsp cider vinegar

1 tsp Dijon mustard

125ml vegetable oil

For the cooked beetroot

Place the different colours of beetroot in separate vacuum pack bags. Split the other ingredients evenly between the two bags and seal. Cook at 85°c for 3 hours in a water bath. Alternatively, rub the beetroot with rapeseed oil and salt, wrap in foil with the thyme and roast in the oven at 150°c for 6-7 hours until soft. Allow to cool, then cut into 3mm slices and cut out discs.

For the pickled beetroot

Place all the ingredients except the beetroot into a saucepan with 150ml of water and bring to the boil, then take off the heat and allow to cool. Peel and thinly slice the beetroot, then cut out small discs. Strain the pickling liquor onto the beetroot discs and allow to pickle for at least 24 hours.

For the bramble ketchup

Sweat the shallot, ginger and garlic in pan with a little oil. Once softened, add the spices and toast for a few minutes. Add the remaining ingredients and simmer until the ketchup has thickened. Blitz until smooth and then allow to cool.

For the hazelnut mayo

First make a hazelnut butter by blending the hazelnuts with a pinch of salt until smooth, scraping the side frequently. The mixture will start out crumbly but will eventually become smooth. Meanwhile, whisk the egg yolks, vinegar and mustard together until combined. Slowly add the oil and 50g of the hazelnut butter to the yolk mixture, whisking continuously until you have a thick mayonnaise.

To assemble and serve

Season and cook the pigeon breasts in a hot pan with oil and butter for around 30 seconds on each side. Add 8 discs of each cooked beetroot to the pan, season with salt and place in an oven at 200°c for 1 minute. Take the pigeon and beetroot out of the pan and rest the pigeon in a warm place for 4 minutes. Place some of the bramble ketchup on a plate, followed by the cooked and pickled beetroot discs. Garnish with the fresh brambles, crushed hazelnuts and hazelnut mayo. Carve the rested pigeon and add to the plate.

A FOOD & DRINK SHOPPING EXPERIENCE

This monthly outdoor market offers an array of quality local produce in the heart of the city.

Perth Farmers' Market, the first one in Scotland, was the idea of local sheep farmer Jim Fairlie. He was inspired by the local markets during a visit to France and in particular the number of small producers selling their own produce grown in the vicinity. His aim was to create a platform in Scotland to give farmers the opportunity to sell their produce directly to customers as an alternative to selling only through the major multiple retailers. The idea became a reality, and the first market took place on 3rd April 1999 on King Edward Street, Perth with just twelve stalls.

The market has gone from strength to strength and now regularly has around fifty stallholders on the first Saturday of every month, showcasing a range of quality local produce. Although at first it was a market mainly for farmers, it has since become more of a producer market and has been able to increase its offering to include things such as chocolate, chilli sauce, gluten-free baking, granola, beer, cider and spirits. Another interesting development has seen the inclusion of an international element with producers using locally sourced ingredients to create products from their original homeland. This includes French, Italian and American bakers and African and Greek cuisine.

In 2020, the market relocated to the South Inch car park just outside the city centre. This has created an even better shopping experience with more space for stalls and a more comfortable environment for customers. With strict guidelines on maintaining the quality of produce on display, customers have confidence that the food and drink they are buying is produced locally and to a high standard by people who care and have pride in what they are offering. Consumers are far more interested now in where their food comes from and how far it has travelled than ever before. This interaction between buyer and producer makes a visit to the market a unique experience that is difficult to replicate in a typical retail environment.

There is always a great atmosphere on market days, with the eagerness of regular shoppers combining with those who like to take their time to browse and look for something that little bit different, perhaps for a special occasion. Visitors turn out whatever the weather to sample the wares, meet up with friends and without doubt take home some of the finest food in Scotland.

PORK MEDALLIONS WITH GIN AND MUSTARD SAUCE

Preparation time: 20 minutes | Cooking time: 45 minutes | Serves 4

This recipe is made using farm-reared rare breed pork, but the meat can be substituted for rose veal escalopes or steak. Likewise, the pumpkin can be substituted for any root vegetables. The rare breed pork is from Good-Life Farming, pumpkin from Bellfield Organics and gin from The Perth Distillery Company.

800g pumpkin
2 shallots
2 Bramley apples
120ml Perth Gin
175g crème fraiche
35g English mustard
600g pork medallions
Salt and pepper
Oil

Preheat the oven to 200°c. Peel the pumpkin and dice into small cubes around 2-3cm. Drizzle with oil, season with salt and pepper to taste, then roast in the oven for around 45 minutes or until golden. Meanwhile, finely chop the shallots and sweat one of them in a saucepan on a medium heat. Peel and chop the apples, add them to the pan with the shallot and stir regularly until the apples become soft. Take off the heat and set aside to cool.

Sweat the remaining shallot in a clean saucepan on a medium heat. Add 115ml of the gin and reduce, then stir in the crème fraiche and English mustard with salt and pepper to taste. Add an additional 2.5ml gin to the sauce just before serving.

Blend the now cooled apple and shallot mixture to a purée with the remaining 2.5ml of Perth Gin. Add a small amount of oil to a frying pan on a high heat. Add the pork medallions and fry until golden in colour, around 5 minutes on each side.

To serve

Place the roasted pumpkin in the centre of a plate with the pork medallions on top and finish with the sauce. Serve with a spoonful of apple and shallot purée on the side.

Apple crisps make a nice optional extra for this dish. Thinly slice an eating apple, lay the slices on a baking tray and place in a preheated oven at 120°c for 20 minutes.

Recipe by Good Life Farming, a regular stall holder at Perth Farmers' Market.

CELEBRATING SCOTTISH FOOD & DRINK

The Pickled Peacock is a delightfully quirky café bar based at Cairn o' Mohr –
Scotland's only mainland winery – that's full of surprises.

Linsay Duncan had been a tour guide at the Cairn o' Mohr winery for seven years when she approached its owners with an exciting new business idea. Having already established her own company, Speak Scotland, to promote the country's food and drink industry which she is so passionate about, Linsay saw huge potential for the perfect synergy between a winery and café bar, so The Pickled Peacock was born. Opening in 2020 meant that her new venture began as a takeaway due to lockdown restrictions, but the amount of support from customers has ensured a booming business since day one.

The cornerstone of the café bar's ethos is to celebrate Scottish food and drink, so the menu naturally features a smorgasbord of local producers. The Gowrie Gaucho, for example, is a hearty breakfast including venison chorizo from Great Glen Charcuterie, black pudding from Yorkes of Dundee (a gluten-free butcher) and chilli jam from Allan's Chilli Products in Abernethy. The Pickled Peacock offers lots of seasonal dishes as the chefs get first pick of the fresh produce often sourced by the winery, alongside many local ingredients from nearby customers' gardens! This approach allows them to stay in touch with the landscape and develop dishes that reflect Perthshire, making the carefully curated menu of brunches, lunches and grazing boards all the more special.

It's not just what you can eat and drink that makes The Pickled Peacock a destination to be experienced; from the artwork covering the walls to the peacock feather table decorations, there's creativity and fun everywhere you look. The unique space is popular for events – tutored wine flights, painting classes and wedding dinners to name just a few – and boasts an outdoor decking area as well as a dog friendly conservatory. It's important to Linsay and her team that, despite its close connection to the winery, The Pickled Peacock is first and foremost a family-friendly eatery. From the playpark on site to the relaxed atmosphere of the café, every aspect is designed to make sure that every visitor is well looked after.

"People spend time absorbing the place and feel that time slows down here," explains Linsay. "We've always encouraged that with our sharing and grazing dishes as well as our warm and friendly service, which is provided by local people who are part of this community and passionate about Perthshire's food and drink." Whether you come for the full winery tour and slap up lunch or simply a summer's evening drink, The Pickled Peacock can't wait to welcome you.

THE PICKLED PEACOCK'S
TASTING EXPERIENCE @cairnomohr

RED WINE   WHITE WINE
BRAMBLE   DRY 13.3% 75cl   SPRING OAK   MED SWEET 13.3% 75cl
ELDERBERRY OAK AGED 13.3% 75cl   AUTUMN OAK   MED DRY 13.3% 75cl
CHERRY   FULL BODIED 13.3% 75cl   ELDERFLOWER   MED SWEET 12.9% 75cl
ROSE   GOOSEBERRY &   MEDIUM 13.5% 75cl
RASPBERRY   ELDERFLOWER
STRAWBERRY
                              CIDER 5%
POM   MIXED FRUIT 4.5%

SPICED VENISON BAZLAMA, BEETROOT HUMMUS & VEGETABLE SLAW

Preparation time: 1 hour 30 minutes | Cooking time: 2 hours 30 minutes | Serves 8

Perthshire is famed for its stunning landscapes and has long since been renowned as 'Scotland's Larder' with its abundance of producers, famers and wild game. Venison deserves to be celebrated and this dish most certainly allows it to take centre stage.

For the roasted venison

1 tsp (each) onion powder, garlic powder, smoked paprika and dried rosemary

1 venison haunch (approx. 1.5-2kg)

For the bazlama (flatbread)

240g plain flour & 7g dry yeast

5g each salt and sugar

90g plain yoghurt

For the beetroot houmous

400g tinned chickpeas

250g cooked beetroot

100ml olive oil

2 tsp tahini

1 tsp garlic purée

Squeeze of lemon juice

For the vegetable slaw

4 carrots & 2 courgettes

1 each celeriac, onion & white cabbage

Fresh parsley, chopped

Mustard seed vinaigrette

For the dip (cacik)

1 cucumber

Good handful of fresh mint and parsley

1 clove of garlic

200g plain yoghurt

Preheat the oven to 250°c. Combine all the dry ingredients for the venison and apply to the meat, rubbing and massaging until well coated. Heat a large pan and sear the venison until coloured all over, then place on a roasting tray. Roast for 30 minutes at 250°c and then reduce the temperature to 230°c for about 2 hours. Once cooked, remove the venison from the oven and leave to rest.

Meanwhile, prepare the bazlama. Mix the flour, yeast, salt and sugar together in a bowl. Add the yoghurt and 85ml of water, then knead until combined. Continue kneading until the dough becomes elasticated. It should not be too sticky. Shape into a ball, cover and leave to sit for an hour to prove. Divide the proved dough into 8 smaller balls, let them rest for a further 10 minutes, then roll each ball into a 15cm diameter flatbread. Heat a dry skillet and cook each flatbread for approximately 45 seconds or until it begins to puff up. Flip over and repeat on the other side.

Place all the houmous ingredients in a blender and blitz until puréed. Season to taste and set aside. Prepare the slaw by shredding or finely chopping all the vegetables. Combine them in a large bowl with the chopped parsley, then drizzle with mustard seed vinaigrette. Mix well and season to taste.

For the dip, roughly chop the cucumber and herbs. Crush the garlic, add everything to the yoghurt and stir to combine.

To serve

Warm the flatbreads and spread them with beetroot houmous. Place the vegetable slaw on top followed by the carved roasted venison. We like to drizzle these with Allan's Bramble and Chilli Sauce and then garnish with pea shoots. Serve the bazlama with your cucumber dip and a glass (or bottle) of Gooseberry and Elderflower Wine.

CALIFORNIA DREAMIN'

Established by husband and wife team Roseanna and Morgwn Preston-Jones, Redwood Wines is a sophisticated and friendly neighbourhood wine shop and bar in the idyllic village of Dunkeld.

Redwood Wines' owners first met a long way from Perthshire. Roseanna and Morgwn Preston-Jones worked together in a small Brooklyn coffee shop while hustling through college and work gigs in New York, but they always dreamt of owning their own business. Fast forward a few years and that dream became a reality when they moved to rural Scotland and brought their shared passion for seasonal food and great wine along with them. Redwood Wines is focused on working with local farms and showcasing produce from small wineries, promoting the wonderful food and drink around Dunkeld where the wine shop and bar has made a home.

For Morgwn and Roseanna, the experience of enjoying wine is very much a family affair and so they wanted to create a culture to reflect that at Redwood Wines. Designed to their personal taste, the sleek, minimal décor pairs with vintage crockery and antique crystal in the warm and inviting space, which also features bar tops made from large slabs of old Scottish oak, sourced locally from Murthly castle estate. As passionate about food as they are about wine, Redwood serves house-made charcuterie, artisanal cheeses, preserves and organic produce from a daily changing menu. The roast beef sandwich has a cult following with locals thanks to the delicious Aberdeen angus beef, roasted daily and piled high on freshly made focaccia.

All the food at Redwood Wines is fresh and local wherever possible, in line with the strong ethos behind the business. Morgwn and Roseanna use Little Trochry Farm for vegetables and herbs, Dunkeld smoked salmon is a lunchtime staple and they even have a little allotment in the village which provides fruits, berries, herbs and flowers for the shop. Drawing inspiration from the seasons, the food offering embraces Perthshire produce alongside the owners' experience of working in many of the biggest culinary cities in the world.

The business name reflects this marriage of local and far-flung influences, chosen for its Californian connection to the giant redwoods and the shop's location in Dunkeld surrounded by lush pine forests. "We often walk the local trails surrounded by these towering trees, discussing and sharing our ideas for the business and relishing in our luck at living in such a beautiful part of Scotland," say Morgwn and Roseanna. The next step for the flourishing venture is an expansion of both the wine tasting program and the shop itself, by renovating the cellar space to host rare wines and a sharing table for intimate gatherings and tastings, so there's plenty more to come!

ROASTED BEETROOT WITH AVOCADO

Preparation time: 15 minutes | Cooking time: 2 hours | Serves 4

I love the combination of flavours in this composed salad. I first learned of this combination when I worked at a restaurant in California that was heavily influenced by Alice Waters. In so many ways it is the best of what a wintry salad aspires to be.

1kg raw beetroot
150ml white wine
30ml sherry vinegar
150ml extra virgin olive oil
1 shallot
1 lime
1 lemon
1 medium orange
2 ripe avocados
50g blanched and roasted hazelnuts
Small bunch of fresh coriander
Sea salt

Wash the beetroot and place into a baking tray. Season with sea salt and add the white wine, cover and roast in a 200°c oven until tender. This will take between 1 and a half to 2 hours. Remove from the oven and let the beetroot cool before peeling the skins off.

Cut the cooled and peeled beetroot into wedges, place in a bowl and toss with 15ml of the sherry vinegar and 50ml of the olive oil to coat. Season the dressed beetroot with sea salt to taste, then set aside to cool completely.

To make the vinaigrette, finely mince the shallot and add to a small bowl. Zest and juice the lime, lemon and orange into the bowl, then add the remaining sherry vinegar and finish the vinaigrette with the remaining olive oil.

To serve

Place a quarter of the beetroot on each plate. Halve the avocados, discarding the pit, and spoon wedges onto the plates. Season the avocado with sea salt and dress the plate generously with the shallot vinaigrette. Crumble the roasted hazelnuts over the top and garnish with coriander leaves.

PORK AND DUCK TERRINE

Preparation time: 30 minutes, plus overnight | Cooking time: 1 hour 10 minutes | Serves 8-10

This is a staple at the shop on our charcuterie board. It's great served cold with a dollop of mustard, cornichons and some crusty bread. The caraway adds a great depth of flavour that compliments the pork and duck.

1kg pork mince (20% fat)

2 duck breasts, cut into 2.5cm dice

40g sea salt

2g ground caraway seeds

1g ground mace

2 whole shallots, finely minced

4 cloves of garlic, finely minced

30g unsalted butter

60g double cream

50g shelled pistachios

40g plain flour

30g pink peppercorns

10g fresh parsley, finely minced

1g fresh thyme, finely minced

2 eggs

Combine the pork mince and diced duck breast with the salt, caraway and mace. Mix to combine and set aside in the fridge to keep cool.

In a pan on medium heat, sweat down the shallots and garlic with the butter until translucent. Set aside to cool completely.

Combine the meat mixture with the cooled shallot mixture and all the remaining ingredients in a mixer for 2 minutes or by hand until homogenous.

Transfer the mixture to a terrine mould and pat down to ensure there are no air pockets. Cover with the terrine mould lid and rest in the fridge for 1 hour.

Meanwhile, preheat the oven to 150°c for at least 20 minutes. Place the terrine in a casserole dish large enough to fit the mould with space around the edges. Bring some water to a boil and pour into the casserole so it comes halfway up the terrine mould to create a water bath.

Cook in the oven for 1 hour until the middle of the terrine registers 65°c. Remove the terrine from the oven, cover the top with parchment and cool before placing in the fridge. Add weights atop the terrine in order to press it overnight before slicing and serving.

GASTRONOMY AT GLENEAGLES

Restaurant Andrew Fairlie is Scotland's only two Michelin star restaurant, based inside the world-famous Gleneagles, a palatial luxury hotel set within the rolling Perthshire hills.

Renowned Perthshire-born chef Andrew Fairlie opened his own restaurant as an independent business within the iconic Gleneagles Hotel in May 2001, becoming the founder of a fine dining destination that has since achieved two Michelin stars and iconic status. Having surrounded himself with likeminded people who shared his desire to create something that could be considered truly world class, Andrew set the benchmark that his team still work towards with the same motivation and ambition he embodied.

Sadly, Andrew passed away in 2019 and head chef Stephen McLaughlin, who had been cooking alongside him since 1995, now runs the kitchen. Dale Dewsbury, who was also part of the team who established Restaurant Andrew Fairlie, is general manager and the longevity of many more committed team members has pushed the restaurant forward over the years. They include sous chef Russell Plowman, restaurant manager Ross Hunter and his assistant John Preston, as well as Samantha Geddes and Frenk Trouw among other key players.

At the heart of the business is great produce cooked with care, skill and passion. The restaurant's style is rooted in classical methods with a nod to modernity, so diners can expect purity of flavour over everything else. It's also known for the warmth and professionalism of the service; neither are new concepts in hospitality, but it takes something special to achieve those high standards with such consistency. Inspired by both Andrew's legacy and Gleneagles itself, the restaurant sits within the heart of the hotel but enjoys an intimate and elegant Art Deco style space, invigorated by a full renovation in 2022.

Both à la carte and degustation menus are offered, featuring dishes that showcase the abundant Scottish larder. With one or two exceptions, all the produce is local or home-grown, including an array of vegetables, fruit, herbs and edible flowers from the restaurant's own 'Secret Garden' which has driven the menu since the team's commitment to growing their own in 2012, alongside Scottish meats, game, fish and shellfish. "The dish that we all love is the Home Smoked Scottish Lobster, finished with a citrus and herb butter. I could talk for hours about it and still not do it justice – so you'll just have to come and eat it!" says head chef Stephen.

The team at Restaurant Andrew Fairlie take tremendous pride in preserving the ethos and vision of its namesake, evidenced by their many accolades over the years but above all by the passion and dedication that goes into the continual evolution of this unique culinary landmark.

RAVIOLI OF PERTHSHIRE CEPS WITH WHITE BEAN VELOUTÉ

Preparation time: 1 hour | Cooking time: 35 minutes | Serves 4

The deep nutty flavour of the warm cep duxelles is beautifully heightened by the creamy, velvety and luxurious white bean velouté in this dish. Top tip: any extra ceps that you are lucky enough to have can be frozen whole and kept for future recipes, same for the pasta dough and duxelles domes.

For the cep duxelles

1kg ceps, foraged from around The King's Course at Gleneagles

1kg button mushrooms

500g Paris browns

Light olive oil

50g unsalted butter

150g shallot, finely chopped

4 plump cloves of garlic, puréed

1 lemon, juiced

Chopped tarragon

For the pasta dough

1160g OO flour

8 eggs

12 yolks

20ml olive oil

2 tbsp water

For the white bean velouté

250g coco beans, soaked in cold water for 12 hours

3 litres good chicken stock

1 bouquet garni

200ml milk

120g unsalted butter

Black truffle, to serve

For the cep duxelles

Wash and pat dry all the mushrooms. Heat a little oil in a suitable pan and fry the mushrooms until the liquid comes out. Tip the mushrooms into a colander and leave to cool, then roughly chop. Wipe the pan and cook the butter until nutty and foamy. Sweat the shallots and garlic without colouring them until softened. Add all the mushrooms and cook on a medium high heat for 7-8 minutes until the mixture is dry. Transfer the mushroom mixture to a food processor, add the lemon juice and pulse to a rough purée. Check the seasoning, add the chopped tarragon, then chill until needed.

For the pasta dough and white bean velouté

Carefully mix all the ingredients together by hand until the mixture forms a smooth, stretchy dough. Wrap in cling film and rest for 1 hour in the fridge. Put the drained beans, stock, and bouquet garni into a suitable pot. Simmer gently until the beans are very tender. Blend to a purée and then push through a fine sieve into a clean pan. Warm the milk, stir it into the bean purée, then add the butter and return the mix to a clean blender. Blend on full power for 2 minutes. Check the seasoning and keep the velouté warm until ready to serve.

To assemble the ravioli

Line a 100ml ladle with a small piece of cling film and neatly overlap the edges. Carefully spoon the chilled duxelles into the ladle, pushing firmly to create a neat shape. Remove from the ladle, peel off the cling film and keep the 'dome' chilled until needed. Repeat until all the duxelles has been used. Very lightly dust a flat work surface with flour, roll out the pasta and cut into discs larger than the duxelles domes. Brush a pasta disc with a few drops of cold water, place a duxelles dome in the centre, then place another disc directly on top and press gently around the dome to seal, eliminating any air pockets as you go. Carefully pick up the ravioli and trim into a neat round shape with sharp kitchen scissors. Repeat to make 16 raviolis. They can be kept in the fridge on a lightly floured plate for up to 4 hours.

To cook and serve

Bring a large saucepan of generously salted water to the boil, carefully add your ravioli and cook for 3 minutes. They should rise to the surface when ready. Carefully transfer the ravioli to a warmed soup plate, then pour the warm velouté around them. Cover the ravioli with freshly shaved black truffle and serve at once. Bon appétit!

NATURAL GOODNESS

Grown, pressed and bottled on the family farm in Perthshire, the award-winning
Summer Harvest Cold Pressed Rapeseed Oil is a true success story.

The beginnings of Summer Harvest took place in the most unlikely setting for a Perthshire rapeseed oil producer: a party in London, where Mark and Maggie met for the first time. They got together, married, worked as an IT consultant and a physiotherapist respectively, then decided to move up to Scotland where Maggie's family lived and farmed. By this point, Mark knew he wanted to work in the food and drink sector, so he started helping his father-in-law on the farm which was growing seed potatoes as part of the crop rotation. The oversized ones couldn't be sold through the usual channels, so Mark spotted an opportunity to try and sell them on a larger scale.

Mark's potato pitch went down a treat with local farm shops and restaurants, and he also managed to secure a farmers' market stall. Unfortunately, the nature of the business meant that while he sold stacks of potatoes, he probably hadn't made a penny, so he continued to look for other ways of adding value to the traditional arable and livestock farm. Mark then heard about UK-grown rapeseed oil, which nobody at the time was producing in Scotland, and decided to give it a go himself. From the very first ton, grown on the family farm, it proved even more popular than potatoes with those same clients he had already built relationships with.

In October 2008, Summer Harvest was established and the rapeseed oil producer has been trading ever since, supplying independent retailers, Scottish Waitrose branches and food service with its flagship product. Mark has broadened the range along the way, adding a truffle-infused oil and a range of salad dressings made in collaboration with prestigious Scottish catering company Wilde Thyme. His ethos has remained true to that first foray into diversification: utilise what you've already got on your own farm to add value, be open and transparent – and above all, make a great product.

Summer Harvest is still family-run and uses a tight-knit structure to keep all developments under Mark's careful eye, ensuring the quality and vision are never compromised. Distribution is now UK-wide although the local independent businesses are still a key part of the network. Restaurant Andrew Fairlie has been a staunch supporter of Summer Harvest since the beginning, which led to the introduction of farm tours so the chefs – and others, including corporate visits and students – can get better acquainted with the product they are cooking with. Mark runs the tours himself and is proud to showcase the business he has built.

HONEY & RAPESEED OIL FLAPJACKS

Preparation time: 15 minutes | Cooking time: 20-25 minutes | Makes 12 bars

Cold Pressed Rapeseed Oil is an extremely versatile oil and can be used in dressings, mayonnaise and roasting. For this recipe, we have married up the oil with the honey produced in our oilseed rape fields and locally grown oats to produce a great snack.

3 tbsp syrup

2 tbsp honey (look for white thick-set honey as this will be from oilseed rape)

120ml Summer Harvest Cold Pressed Rapeseed Oil

200g porridge oats (we use Gloagburn Farm Shop porridge flakes)

Optional Extras

25g sunflower seeds

110g chopped walnuts

110g dried cranberries

The secret to flapjacks is to make sure you have all your ingredients and utensils ready before you start cooking. For this recipe, we have chosen sunflower seeds, walnuts and cranberries, but you can use any combination of dried fruit, seeds and nuts. Or just use what you have in the store cupboard. Preheat the oven to 200°c or 180°c fan. Grease and line a 9 inch square baking tray, then measure out all your ingredients. Perhaps get your children to help to weigh out the ingredients – I would say this could save you time, but I know the truth...

Next, select your saucepan wisely as there is a fair bit of mixing to do and you don't want any spillages. In the well-selected saucepan, melt the syrup and honey with the oil over a moderate heat.

When the honey and syrup have melted, add all the dry ingredients to the saucepan and thoroughly mix, making sure every bit is coated with the oil mixture.

Place the mixture into the lined tin and press down firmly, ensuring the mixture is flat and even. Cook in the preheated oven for around 20 minutes. The flapjacks will be ready when the edges turn a golden colour.

Do not remove the flapjacks from the tin at this stage; leave them to cool down for an hour or two, then once cooled remove from the baking tin and cut into slices.

Enjoy as a mid-morning snack, perhaps with a dollop of crème fraiche along with a cup of Glen Lyon coffee. They are also great as a snack while out walking the hills of Perthshire.

SPICE UP YOUR LIFE!

Tabla is an authentic Indian dining experience based in Perth, combining the best produce from around the UK with spices grown on the owners' family farms in India to create delicious dishes for the restaurant, takeaway, cook school and Curry Club within their thriving family business.

Tabla was founded by Praveen and Swarna Kumar with the aim of introducing more authentic Indian food to Perthshire. Having both grown up in rural Indian villages, where every meal was freshly prepared from ingredients grown in the surrounding fields, the couple wanted to bring that approach to their adopted home of Scotland. The result is a homely yet delicious dining experience that has garnered local and national acclaim since opening in 2009 on Perth's South Street.

The restaurant's ethos is based around simple, tasty food that uses what is available in the surrounding area. Most of the meat and seafood is sourced from Perthshire while the vegetables are grown by Farmer John at Tabla Market Garden. Spices are the exception, as they are grown in Praveen's own family fields back in India. With dishes based on British produce including lamb from Dundee and chicken from Cumbria, the à la carte menu changes with the seasons and is renowned for the street food style starters. More adventurous than your typical bhajis and pakoras, it includes haggis bonda, Indian spiced fried fish and tandoori salmon alongside a wide variety of main courses that blend northern and southern Indian influences.

Featuring an open kitchen, stone walls and a modern but cosy feel, Tabla has an ambience to match the quality of its food. The building dates back to 1840 and has been decorated to reveal plenty of character, while Praveen's extensive experience in hospitality – including as the restaurant manager for Gleneagles and Turnberry Hotels in Scotland – ensures that the service is always spot on. Such attention to detail across all areas of the business has been rewarded with an AA Rosette, Scottish Chef of the Year and many other accolades over the years.

"Tabla stands out because we don't just serve any Indian food – it's top quality and that's what people come here for because they know we are providing that same experience that we would expect to find back home in India," says Praveen. The restaurant also offers takeaway and home delivery alongside a newer aspect of the business: Kumar's Curry Club. Founded by Praveen, the meal box service aims to ensure that anyone can enjoy healthy, authentic Indian cuisine. In combination with their Indian Cook School, which is also based in Perth and offers a masterclass with Praveen and Swarna, the Kumars are proud to be changing the landscape of Indian food in Scotland.

CHICKEN BHUNA

Preparation time: 1 hour 30 minutes | Cooking time: 20-25 minutes | Serves 2

This bhuna recipe is very versatile and can be made with chicken, lamb, prawns or vegetables.
Add single cream or coconut cream for a richer dish.

350g chicken breast, cubed (or your choice of protein/vegetables)

1 tbsp ginger-garlic paste

½ tsp each of chilli powder, garam masala and curry powder

Rapeseed oil

Salt, to taste

4 cloves of garlic, diced

½ inch fresh ginger, diced

½ tsp each of coriander, cumin and mustard seeds

1 whole green chilli (optional)

1 large onion, diced

1 large tomato, diced

Mix the chicken with the ginger-garlic paste, ground spices and a little rapeseed oil to make a paste. Season with salt and marinate for 1 hour.

Heat a medium saucepan on high heat. Add enough oil to the pan to cover the base. Add the diced garlic and ginger and fry until golden, about 1 minute.

Add the whole spices and green chilli (if using) to the pan and fry for 30 seconds. Add the diced onions and continue frying until they are brown all over, stirring regularly.

Once the onions are brown, add the diced tomato. Boil for 5 minutes until the tomatoes are soft. Add the chicken and marinade to the pan, topping up with water to cover the meat.

Simmer for 15 minutes (or if you are using lamb, simmer for 1 hour until tender). Season with salt to taste, then enjoy!

A HOMEGROWN FOOD & MUSIC DESTINATION

Set on the banks of the River Tay in historic Dunkeld, The Taybank is a food, travel, arts and culture destination at the heart of a thriving creative community.

In late 2019, Dunkeld local Fraser Potter took over The Taybank, shortly before the Covid-19 pandemic shut businesses across the country. Using his experience working in events and pop-ups, he transformed what was an unused space in front of the building into Perthshire's biggest riverside beer garden, complete with its own kitchen, bar, coffee and ice cream shack.

When the building remained shut due to social distancing, people came to the gardens to reconnect with friends and enjoy food and drinks in the sun with views of Thomas Telford's famous arched bridge over the Tay. During this time, Fraser also renovated five derelict rooms in the building, turning them into thoughtfully designed ensuite bedrooms. Painted in calming, earthy tones, the rooms are adorned with handpicked mid-century furniture, comfy beds, linens and sheepskins.

Upstairs, overlooking the river and gardens, is The Taybank's atmospheric restaurant. A handmade bar built by local carpenter Angus Ross stocks dozens of Scottish beers, IPAs, ciders and a carefully curated selection of wines. The kitchen and front-of-house team, led by passionate general manager Fran Rossi, run a busy and energetic service all throughout the year. The restaurant's inventive, seasonal menu focuses on homegrown produce from The Taybank's own walled garden in the nearby Murthly Castle Estate along with quality Scottish meat and seafood. Venison, pheasant and other game is responsibly sourced from country estates in and around Dunkeld and fresh seafood arrives daily from a sustainable, family-run fishing business based on the west coast.

Paying homage to the Taybank's musical roots, Fraser, Fran and team also run weekly live music sessions in the famous downstairs bar and larger events such as open-air cinema screenings, parties and festivals in the gardens.

Picture: Richard Gaston

ure: Kimberley Grant

INDIVIDUAL BEETROOT AND WHIPPED GOAT'S CHEESE TARTS

Preparation time: 15 minutes | Cooking time: 50 minutes | Serves 8

We've created a dish that not only has the perfect balance of sweetness and acidity, but also uses beetroot that we grow in our own walled garden. This is a perfect starter for a dinner party, showcasing two wonderful ingredients which speak for themselves.

For the shortcrust pastry

500g flour

1 tsp salt

250g cold butter

2 egg yolks

2 tbsp ice cold water

For the beetroot jam

3 red onions, finely diced

500g fresh beetroot, finely diced

200g sugar

400ml red wine vinegar

150ml red wine

5 juniper berries, crushed

3 sprigs of thyme

For the whipped goat's cheese

250g soft goat's cheese

50g cream cheese

1 lemon, juiced

2 tbsp water

To serve

Pickled beetroot

Chopped chives

For the shortcrust pastry

Sift the flour and salt into a food processor. Add the cold butter and pulse until it resembles breadcrumbs. Add 1 of the egg yolks mixed with the water and lightly pulse until the dough starts to come together. Continue to add 1 tablespoon of water at a time if necessary. Very lightly knead the pastry into a ball, cover with cling film and leave to rest in the fridge for a minimum of 30 minutes.

For the beetroot jam

Fry the red onions in a pan over a low heat for 5-10 minutes until translucent. Add the diced beetroot to the pan and cook for a minute before adding the remaining ingredients. Bring to the boil and then turn down to a gentle simmer. After around 50 minutes, the liquid should have reduced to a syrup. Cook until it reaches a jammy consistency, stirring occasionally to ensure it doesn't burn.

For the whipped goat's cheese

Place all the ingredients except the water in a food processor and whizz on full speed until it forms soft peaks. Add the water if necessary to reach the right consistency.

To assemble the tarts

Roll out the chilled pastry on a lightly floured surface to about 3mm thick. Using a round cutter bigger than the tartlet cases, cut out 8 circles. Working quickly, lay the pastry over the individual tartlet cases and use your fingers to press into the corners and up the sides. Use a sharp knife to trim off the excess. Chill for 30 minutes in the fridge.

Preheat the oven to 170°c fan. Prick the chilled pastry cases all over with a fork. Cut out circles of parchment paper big enough to cover them, scrunch the paper so it fits in more snugly and weigh down with ceramic baking beans. Blind bake in the preheated oven for around 15-20 minutes, then remove the parchment and baking beans, place back in the oven and bake for a further 10 minutes until the base is cooked or a golden brown. It should have a 'sandy' feel when you touch it. Brush with the remaining egg yolk and return to the oven for 5 minutes. Set aside until cool.

Spoon the beetroot jam into the pastry cases and bake at 160°c for 5-10 minutes. Once warm, pipe the whipped goat's cheese on top of each tartlet. Garnish with pickled beetroot and chopped chives.

HALIBUT, SURF CLAMS, CARAMELISED CHICORY & FENNEL

Preparation time: 15 minutes | Cooking time: 45 minutes | Serves 4

This is a simple but delicious dish that showcases both the produce grown in our own walled garden and the best of Scottish seafood perfectly. It uses simple techniques but excellent ingredients to create something that is more than the sum of its parts and perfect for many different occasions.

2 heads of chicory

2 bulbs of fennel

1 orange, zested and juiced

2 tbsp cider vinegar

2 tbsp honey

2 sprigs of thyme

Large knob of butter

Salt, pepper and sumac to taste

4 x 120g halibut fillets

2 tbsp vegetable oil

Drizzle of olive oil

Fresh lemon juice

200ml Breton cider

Handful of surf clams

500ml double cream

Small bunch of parsley, chopped

For the caramelised chicory and fennel

Preheat your oven to 185°c. Halve the chicory, cut the fennel into 5mm slices and add both to a roasting tray. Add the orange zest and juice, cider vinegar, honey, thyme and butter with a pinch of salt and pepper. Wrap the tray tightly in foil and roast for 30 minutes. Remove the foil, turn the veg and roast uncovered for another 15 minutes, until caramelised and the chicory is tender when pierced with a knife.

Meanwhile, preheat a heavy-bottomed frying pan on a medium-high heat. Season the halibut fillets all over with salt and sumac. When the pan is hot, add the vegetable oil and place the halibut carefully into the pan. The fillets will take around 3 minutes per side to cook but depending on thickness may take longer. When you flip them after 3 minutes, they should have a light brown colour on one side and a noticeable 'seam' where the fish is beginning to flake – these are great signs to look out for!

Once the halibut is cooked, carefully transfer it to a warm plate. Drizzle the fillets with a small amount of olive oil and lemon juice, then cover with foil while you cook the clams.

Place the halibut pan on a high heat and add the Breton cider. When this comes to a boil, add the clams and cover the pan with a lid. Cook for approximately 2 minutes or until the clams have all opened, then add the double cream and chopped parsley, removing the pan from the heat.

To serve

Lay the caramelised chicory slightly off centre in a large pasta bowl, then lay the fennel alongside it to create a bed for the halibut. Carefully place the halibut fillets on top of the fennel, arrange the clams around the plate and pour over the cider cream sauce to finish.

RHUBARB AND CARDAMOM COMPOTE

Preparation time: 5 minutes | Cooking time: 25 minutes | Serves 4

This compote strikes the ideal balance between tart and sweet, and can be easily adjusted to suit different palates. We make it from rhubarb picked from The Taybank's walled garden.

500g rhubarb, cut into 5cm sticks
2 blood oranges, zested and juiced
1 vanilla pod, split
80g sugar
10 cardamom seeds, crushed
2 tbsp water
2 tbsp maple syrup

Preheat the oven to 200°c and arrange the rhubarb on a roasting tray lined with baking paper.

Scatter over the orange zest and vanilla seeds, then drop the pod on top. Mix the sugar with the crushed cardamom seeds, then sprinkle it over the rhubarb. Pour over the water and half of the orange juice.

Roast in the preheated oven for 25 minutes or until the rhubarb is soft but holds its shape. Leave to cool, then remove the vanilla pod.

Stir the maple syrup through the rhubarb mixture and taste. If the compote is too sweet, add more orange juice. If it's too tart, add more syrup. Spoon into a jar to store.

We like to serve this compote with our homemade granola and Katy Rodger's natural yoghurt as part of our delicious breakfast hampers, for our guests to enjoy in our bedrooms at The Taybank.

PERTHSHIRE'S DELIGHTFUL DELI

Boasting over thirty food brands produced in Perthshire, The Courtyard Shop is a haven for anyone after a true taste of Scotland.

The Courtyard Shop, situated in picturesque Kenmore, was established to offer its customers the very best Scottish food and drink available in the area. It also boasts a selection of books, gifts and clothing which caters for all ages. Kenmore is always very busy in the summertime, particularly since the huge increase in staycations following the pandemic, so the shop very quickly grew arms and legs to help cope with the seasonality challenges faced by many Scottish rural businesses. Lockdown had everyone cooking or baking for themselves, but holidaymakers are now happier choosing ready-made fresh or frozen meals based on the huge selection the shop has to choose from.

The Courtyard also introduced a takeaway coffee and snack counter, an ice cream parlour, a home delivery service and an online hamper business sending products all over Britain for next day delivery. Most recently, they started making their own Loch Tay Soft Fudge which is sold on site as well as in other shops throughout Scotland. All these activities have helped to bolster the quieter times and ensure the shop is open every day except Christmas and Boxing Day.

The shop is modern and airy and has an atmosphere all its own, generated by an eclectic mix of background music and the hustle and bustle of both locals and holidaymakers taking advantage of the many tastings which are available in the shop on a daily basis. "We are very lucky to have such lovely customers who are always happy to find themselves back in Kenmore," says owner Henry Murdoch. The team is small and very well established, with some members having been there since the shop opened, so they have a wealth of knowledge between them, not only about the products but the local area, too, which they are very proud of.

Kenmore is situated in the heart of Highland Perthshire and is very popular with walkers, cyclists, golfers, paddleboarders and wild swimmers. It is a great base camp from which to go out and explore the local area and enjoy all the activities and attractions it has to offer. After a busy day, many visitors return to the shop to stock up for their evening meals or enjoy a large sugar cone ice cream which the shop has become very well known for. It's also a test of anyone's willpower to walk past the fudge-laden table by the front door without stopping and scooping up at least one of the brightly coloured bags!

SOY CHICKEN FRIED RICE

Preparation time: 15 minutes | Cooking time: 25 minutes | Serves 4

A midweek must for those who love a treat but don't have a lot of time. This tasty Asian-inspired meal
is easy to put together for results that will please everyone.

2 tbsp extra virgin olive oil

3 chicken breasts

Sea salt

Freshly ground black pepper

2 tbsp sesame oil, divided

1 medium onion, chopped

2 carrots, peeled and diced

3 cloves of garlic, minced

1 tbsp freshly minced ginger

250g long grain white rice

200g frozen peas

3 large eggs, beaten

3 tbsp light soy sauce

2 spring onions, thinly sliced

In a large flat pan over a medium heat, heat the olive oil. Season the chicken with salt and pepper on both sides, then place them in the pan and cook until golden. This should take 8 minutes per side and if you have a temperature probe, the chicken should reach 165°c. Remove from the skillet and rest for 5 minutes, then cut into bite-size pieces.

In the same flat pan, heat 1 tablespoon of sesame oil. Add the onion and carrots and cook until soft (about 5 minutes) then add the garlic and ginger. Cook until fragrant for 1 more minute.

Cook the rice in a separate pan until fluffy, then add it to the flat pan along with the peas and cook for 2 minutes until warmed through.

Push the rice to one side of the pan and add the remaining sesame oil to the other side. Add the beaten egg and stir until almost fully cooked, then fold the eggs into rice. Add the diced chicken to the pan with the soy sauce and sliced onions. Stir to combine everything and serve hot.

SUNDAY STRAWBERRY SUNDAE

Preparation time: 15 minutes | Serves 2

This burst of colour in a glass sums up what The Courtyard Shop is all about. Local fresh fruit, Scottish ice cream, giant meringues and homemade soft fudge. Almost too good to eat!

4 wafer tubes

10g white chocolate

1 tbsp hundreds and thousands

400g strawberries

50g caster sugar

2 scoops of strawberry ice cream

2 scoops of vanilla ice cream

Skooshy dairy cream

100g Strawberry and Cream Loch Tay Soft Fudge

1 large vanilla meringue, broken up

6 sprigs of mint (optional)

Icing sugar, to dust

Place the wafer tubes on a tray or plate lined with baking paper. Melt the white chocolate in a bowl over a small pan of simmering water, stirring frequently, then spoon it over one end of the wafers. Before the chocolate sets, sprinkle over the hundreds and thousands until the chocolate is coated with them. Leave to set on baking paper for at least 10 minutes in a cool place.

Meanwhile, blitz half the strawberries (using the larger ones) with the caster sugar in a food processor or with a stick blender to a smooth sauce. Strain the sauce through a sieve into a bowl, then chill until ready to serve. Cut the remaining berries into halves, or quarters if large.

Layer up the ice cream and strawberries with the strawberry sauce in a tall sundae glass. Add the skooshy cream, chunks of fudge, pieces of meringue and mint leaves (if using). Top with a halved strawberry and the chocolate dipped wafers, then dust with icing sugar and serve immediately.

WHERE FIELD MEETS FORK

Situated within a stunning Aberfeldy hill farm, Thyme Deli & Bistro at Errichel offers relaxed dining, shopping and farm stays. Run by husband-and-wife team Paul and Becky, the venue is loved for its mix of local and farm-reared produce – with a dash of international inspiration from Paul's years as a globetrotting chef.

Situated on a working rare-breed hill farm above Aberfeldy in Highland Perthshire, Thyme Deli & Bistro at Errichel is the brainchild of chef Paul Newman and wife Becky Newman. Paul and Becky aim to make Errichel a key foodie destination within Perthshire through everything they do. With the produce of the farm utilised in the creations of chef Paul and his team, Errichel has become known as the place 'where field meets fork'.

Guests love the informal dining overlooking sweeping Tay Valley views, deli shopping in the former farmhouse kitchen and comfortable, stylish accommodation. Farm tours, guided personally by Becky, offer a chance to meet Errichel's ethically reared rare-breed animals and explore its slow food philosophy, as well as to hear tales of mad geese and wayward goats! Chef Paul's award-winning foods can be purchased on-site and online, continuing the experience after you've left. For those wishing to take a deeper dive into Scotland's artisan food scene, guided food tastings focusing on Scottish cheeses or charcuterie are a tempting way to spend an afternoon.

Having worked internationally for many years, particularly on the continent of Africa, Paul's ethos for Thyme Bistro's eclectic but unpretentious menu is 'locally sourced, globally inspired'. Brunch classics like Club Sandwiches happily rub shoulders with a richly flavoured venison tagine, and Ghanian Peanut Curry is served as a 'Bunny Chow' in a crusty roll.

The bistro is located within Errichel's beautiful stone 'roundhouse' – a faithful recreation of a typical Scottish horse-mill. Extended over the years from a small farmhouse, Errichel continues to evoke Scotland's agricultural heritage through its beautiful stone and woodwork, but don't be surprised to see more exotic additions like African sculptures and Asian artefacts, giving the interior an unusual and intriguing ambience.

This approach continues in Paul's artisan fine food range of chutneys, pickles and preserves, where meticulously sourced core ingredients are given a deliciously offbeat twist using Paul's deft touch with flavour. Paul's authentic South African biltong utilises the ethically reared, grass-fed beef of Errichel's small herd of Shetland cows. Much of the range has scooped Great Taste awards, with a growing number given the highest honour of three stars. Having been the recipient of several personal awards, in 2022 Paul was named Scotland's Sustainable Chef of the Year by the Rare Breeds Survival Trust.

VENISON TAJINE

Preparation time: 30 minutes | Cooking time: 3 hours | Serves 4

Paul learned the secret to making tajines while working as a chef in North Africa. This version utilises
the iconic Scottish wild venison which roam freely across the farm. Delicious year-round but coming
into its own in autumn and winter, this has become a Thyme Bistro signature dish.

600g wild Perthshire venison, diced

1 red onion

½ a bunch of fresh coriander

Olive oil

400g dried chickpeas, soaked overnight (or 1 tin)

400g fresh plum tomatoes, diced

800ml vegetable stock

800g butternut squash

600g sweet potato

100g toffee dates

100g dried apricots

1 tbsp fig syrup

1 tbsp prune syrup

For the spice rub

1 level tbsp (each) ras el hanout, ground cumin, ground cinnamon, ground coriander, sweet paprika, ground ginger, za'atar, green thyme, chopped garlic, chopped red or green standard chillies

For the garnish

2 tbsp flaked almonds

20g sliced green pistachios

Fresh pomegranate seeds

2 fresh figs, sliced

Greek yoghurt

Mix all the spice rub ingredients together in a small bowl with a good pinch of sea salt and black pepper, then gently cook in a frying pan for 3-4 minutes without browning, just to allow the spice oils and flavours to develop.

Place the diced venison into a large bowl and mix it with the toasted spice rub, then cover with cling film and place in the fridge for a couple of hours, preferably overnight.

When you're ready to cook, peel and finely chop the red onion, then pick the coriander leaves, finely chopping the stalks. Heat a generous amount of olive oil in a tajine (make sure your dish is suitable for the stove top and/or oven, as some are just for serving in) or casserole pan over a medium heat. Add the marinated venison and fry to seal and colour the meat. Add the onion and coriander stalks and fry for a further 5 minutes.

Drain and tip in the chickpeas, followed by the tomatoes, breaking them up with a spoon, then pour in 400ml of the stock and stir well. Bring to the boil, then cover and reduce to a low heat for 1 hour 30 minutes. Meanwhile, deseed and chop the squash into 5cm chunks, cut the sweet potato to the same size, then de-stone and roughly tear the dates. Toast the almonds for the garnish in a dry frying pan until lightly golden, then tip into a bowl.

When the time's up, add the squash, sweet potato, dates, apricots and remaining stock to the tajine. Give everything a gentle stir, then pop the lid back on and continue cooking for another 1 hour 30 minutes. Keep an eye on it, adding splashes of water if needed.

At this stage, remove the lid and check the consistency. If it seems a bit too runny, simmer for 5-10 more minutes with the lid off. The venison should be really tender and flaking apart by now, so have a taste and season again if necessary. Add the fig and prune syrups to the mix and simmer for another 2 minutes.

Scatter the coriander leaves over the tagine along with the toasted almonds, pistachios and a handful of pomegranate seeds. Top with the fresh sliced figs. Serve the tajine with a big bowl of lightly seasoned couscous and a dollop of Greek yoghurt, then dive in. You've earned it!

BEETROOT CURED SCOTTISH SALMON

Preparation time: 48 hours | Cooking time: 30 minutes | Serves 4

This is Paul's party piece: a sweet, tangy and succulent alternative to smoked salmon. We usually use 12-year-old Dewar's Scotch whisky in the second cure, which imparts a delicious richness to the final flavour. This is a great starter or buffet piece for dinner parties and can be made well in advance.

For the first cure

250g coarse kosher salt
200g granulated sugar
150g chopped dill
1kg best Scottish fillet salmon, pin bones removed and skin on

For the second cure

200g coarse kosher salt
100g granulated sugar
100g minced fresh beetroot
120g chopped tarragon
120g chopped dill
15g grated horseradish
3 oranges, zested and juiced
100ml good scotch whisky

For the salad
(use any of the following)

Lightly boiled fine green beans
Soft-boiled free-range eggs
Boiled new potatoes
Green and red chicory endive
Samphire
Caperberries
Artichokes
Pea shoots
Cherry tomatoes
Chermoula dressing

Mix the salt, sugar and chopped dill for the first cure. Lay cling film over your work surface and spread half the salt mix on top. Place the fish on top and cover with the remaining salt mix. Wrap in the cling film fairly tightly and place into a metal container. Leave in the fridge for 24 hours.

Wash the first cure off the salmon and pat it dry. Place all the ingredients for the second cure together in a bowl and mix well. As before, lay cling film over your surface and sprinkle half the mix on top, then place the salmon on that and cover with the remaining cure. Fold the cling film tightly over the fish and leave in the fridge for a further 24 hours.

Wash off the second cure. You can enjoy the salmon now or wrap and store it in a container in the fridge for up to 2 weeks. When you are ready to eat the cured salmon, slice thinly from the tail end working up the side.

To serve, build a salad with the ingredients of your choice and slices of your cured salmon. Drizzle with the chermoula dressing and serve immediately.

RISING TO THE OCCASION

Driven by its founder's passion for great food, Wild Hearth Bakery is on a mission to produce Scotland's best sourdough bread and pastries, all with organic flours grown and milled in the UK.

Wild Hearth Bakery is the lifelong dream of John Castley, an artisan baker originally from Australia. Growing up in Sydney with his Hungarian mother and restaurateur grandfather, John was always surrounded by good food. In 2010, he left his IT career to retrain as a chef at Ballymalloe Cookery School in Ireland and fulfil his passion for food in all its forms. After five years cheffing in London, the wildness and beauty of Perthshire drew John to set up his bakery in the village of Comrie.

At the heart of Wild Hearth Bakery is a 14-ton wood oven, fired exclusively with sawmill waste. The name reflects the wildness of its location surrounded by stunning mountains, the wild sourdough culture which is used in all their products and the hearth or fireplace which transforms a raw dough into beautiful bread. Wild Hearth can also claim to be the only wood-fired sourdough bakery located in Nissen Hut in a World War Two prisoner of war camp!

Local and responsible sourcing of ingredients is a very important part of Wild Hearth's ethos. These include rye flour from Scotland The Bread in Fife, cultured butter from Edinburgh Butter Company, organic stoneground flour from Yorkshire Organic Millers and single origin bean-to-bar chocolate from Pump Street Chocolate in Suffolk. On the bread front, their 'white' sourdough (actually 25% wholemeal) is still the biggest seller. However, John is on a mission to educate people about the flavour and health benefits of breads made with wholemeal flour, and sales of these are catching up fast. Other firm favourites are the sourdough Danish pastries made with local seasonal fruit and feather-light sourdough bomboloni (Italian doughnuts) filled with a zesty lemon crème pâtissiere.

Fun, humour and a healthy lifestyle are at the heart of the Wild Hearth workplace. Bakers sit down every day to a cooked meal using vegetables grown at the local organic market garden, and all baking shifts are during daytime hours. John credits Hamish, his head of operations, with the commitment and 'can do' approach that keeps the business running smoothly. Wild Hearth has won the last three Scottish Bread Championships in 2019, 2021 and 2022 as well as Slow Food Scottish Bakery of the Year 2022 and first place in the Artisan Food category of the Scottish Rural Awards 2018. They are currently in the process of doubling the size of their wholesale bakery and opening a shop, so there's plenty more innovation and inspiration to come from this Scottish success story.

SCOTTISH SOURDOUGH RYE LOAF

Preparation time: 2 hours | Cooking time: 45 minutes | Makes 2 x 960g loaves

This wholemeal rye bread is delicious, nutritious, easy to make with no kneading involved, and will keep in your kitchen for a week. It can be made with any rye flour, but we use wholemeal rye organically grown and milled in Fife by Scotland The Bread.

For the starter

90g wholemeal rye starter
300g wholemeal rye flour
300g water

For the pre-cooked flour

70g wholemeal rye flour
210g water
18g sea salt

For the final dough

620g wholemeal rye flour
690g wholemeal rye starter (see above)
298g pre-cooked flour (see above)
315g hot water

The night before, mix your starter and make your pre-cooked flour. Mix the starter ingredients together and leave to ferment in a warm place (ideally 24-28°c) for 12-16 hours. You need a live sourdough starter to build from. Get this from a friend, a local bakery, or you can buy some from Scotland The Bread. We give out free starter to anyone who comes to the bakery.

For the pre-cooked flour, measure the flour, water and sea salt into a saucepan and whisk until no lumps remain. Place on a high heat and whisk continuously until it thickens, then take the pan off the heat, cover and cool overnight.

The next day, prepare 2 x 1lb loaf tins. Unless they have a non-stick coating, you will need to grease them. We find that an oil spray (without synthetic additives) is best for this, or you can lightly and evenly butter them as you would a cake tin.

Measure the wholemeal rye flour into a mixing bowl, then add the starter, pre-cooked flour and hot water straight from the tap. Hold your nerve; it feels wrong to do this, but it will achieve a final dough temperature of about 35°c, which is perfect.

Mix with a wooden spoon for about a minute, or until smooth. The consistency will be more like a thick batter than a typical bread dough. Divide the dough evenly between the tins, trying not to smear it down the sides, as this can result in the bread sticking.

Sift a thin layer of rye flour over each loaf and leave to rise in a warm place (28-34°c) for about 1 hour 30 minutes until the rye flour on top has cracked and darker bubbles are visible through the cracks. It's not necessary to cover them. The loaves should still be a bit domed when they go in the oven; if they have begun to collapse then the dough has overproved. Meanwhile, preheat your oven to 250°c or 230°c fan.

Bake the loaves in the preheated oven for 10 minutes and then reduce the temperature to 220°c or 200°c fan and bake for a further 30-35 minutes. The internal temperature should reach 97°c.

Remove the loaves from the tins and allow to cool. This bread is the perfect accompaniment to smoked salmon, ideally with some pickled vegetables, crème fraiche and fresh dill.

SHOWCASING SCOTLAND'S SEASONAL LARDER

For delicious set menus or private dining for special events and a contemporary Perthshire experience, 63 Tay Street should be top of your list.

63 Tay Street is an award-winning restaurant in Perth that was created to unpretentiously showcase the Scottish seasonal larder in relaxed and inviting surroundings. Chef patron Graeme Pallister follows this guiding principle to create dishes that allow the ingredients to do the talking. Both Graeme and the restaurant manager, Christopher Strachan, are Perthshire born and bred so representing the county with pride is important to them. The small team at 63 Tay Street are passionate about using the best quality ingredients from local suppliers according to their mantra of 'Local, Honest, Simple' which defines the restaurant's ethos.

There are two menus to choose from, both carefully curated to showcase this ethos: the four-course lunch option, which is also served on Wednesday and Thursday evenings, has gathered quite a following thanks to its excellent value and the luxurious option of a paired wine flight. The most popular and refined dining experience is the five-course set menu, served on Friday and Saturday evenings also with a wine flight available. Dishes vary throughout the seasons but might include delights such as foraged gooseberry gazpacho, duck haggis pie and milk chocolate mousse with raspberry crowdie.

Scottish suppliers and producers are central to this approach, from Stornoway black pudding to meat from Henderson's butchers and Gloagburn Farm eggs. Their wine supplier, Raeburn Fine Wines, helps Christopher to curate a wide range of wines and aperitifs with a focus on sustainability, provenance, quality and drinkability. There's also plenty of Scottish whisky and other spirits to sip after your meal, including Highland, Lowland, Speyside and Islay single malts to choose from.

Situated on the banks of the River Tay with stunning views across Kinnoull Hill, 63 Tay Street was established in 2007 and has maintained two AA rosettes ever since. It has also been awarded Scottish Restaurant of the Year twice among many other accolades, both local and national. The restaurant can host private parties in an elegantly designed room which offers a beautiful backdrop for celebrations including wedding breakfasts.

With an unwavering commitment to both the guests and the food, 63 Tay Street is the product of chef patron Graeme's passion for local and seasonal produce which results in delicious menus that truly reflect the surrounding county and the rest of Scotland's inimitable larder.

BRAISED PORK NECK IN CABBAGE WITH WHITE BEAN PISTOU

Preparation time: 1-2 hours | Cooking time: 3-4 hours | Serves 6-8

This is another one of my one-pot wonders; life is too short for washing dishes. Although this one demands a little attention from you budding chefs, the result is sublime and the aromas seeping through the kitchen will test your willpower no end – I dare you not to lick the oven!

50g unsalted butter

2 tbsp olive oil

1k boneless pork neck

Salt and pepper

Pinch of Chinese five spice

2 carrots, peeled and halved

2 onions, peeled and halved

3 cloves of garlic, halved with the germ removed

1 sprig of rosemary

1 sprig of thyme

250g dried haricot beans, soaked overnight

2 rashers of grilled bacon

2 fresh bay leaves

1.5 litres chicken stock (fresh or with stock cubes)

Handful of fresh basil leaves

1 tbsp toasted pine nuts

1 tbsp finely grated parmesan

2 tbsp extra virgin olive oil

1 large Savoy cabbage

2 tbsp double cream

You will need a large pan with a tight-fitting lid, one that will be good for the hob and oven. Place this on the hob and melt the butter in the olive oil until lightly browned. Season the pork neck all over with plenty of salt, pepper and the five spice. Carefully brown the pork all over in the hot pan; this may take up to 15 minutes.

Remove the pork and immediately add the vegetables, garlic and herbs. Cook for a further 5 minutes, allowing them to caramelise slightly, then add the drained haricot beans, bacon, bay leaves and stock. Place the pork back into the pan. Very slowly bring up to a simmer, place a lid on the pan and braise slowly in a moderate oven for approximately 2 hours 30 minutes. Check halfway through that you have enough liquid, adding boiling water if needed.

Meanwhile, make the pesto by blending the basil, pine nuts, parmesan and olive oil in a food processor or hand-chopping finely with a pinch of salt to taste. Remove the outer leaves of the cabbage, blanch until softened in boiling salted water and immediately cool in iced water. Dry off, remove the centre stalk and cut neat circles out of each leaf.

Once the pork is cooked, allow to cool then roughly chop. Gently massage the meat with some of the stock and roll into balls. Place a square of cling film on a board, add an upturned cabbage leaf on top and place a ball of pork in the middle. Wrap the cabbage firmly around the pork, trim any excess cabbage and secure with the cling film into a ball.

Remove the vegetables and herbs from the beans, reserving the vegetables. In a separate pan, add the cream to 1 pint of the stock and reduce slightly. Reserve the remaining stock. Chop the vegetables into the creamy sauce and add enough beans to thicken it. Warm the cabbage parcels in a pan of water, then remove the cling film and top with the basil pesto as shown. Enjoy!

The absolute best thing about this dish is that leftovers can be chilled and used later in the week. Chop, bung together and reheat in the extra stock for an amazing rustic soup.

DIRECTORY

63 TAY STREET RESTAURANT

63 Tay Street, Perth, Scotland, PH2 8NN
Telephone: 01738 441451
Website: www.63taystreet.com
Email: info@63taystreet.com
Award-winning restaurant unpretentiously showcasing the Scottish seasonal larder in relaxed and inviting surroundings.

ABERFELDY WATERMILL

Watermill, Mill Street, Aberfeldy, PH15 2BG
Telephone: 01887 822896
Website: www.aberfeldywatermill.com
Email: info@aberfeldywatermill.com
Instagram @aberfeldywatermill
Facebook: Aberfeldy Watermill – Bookshop, Cafe & Art Gallery
Award-winning bookshop, art gallery, cafe and home interiors located in rural Perthshire.

BALLINTAGGART

Ballintaggart Farm, Grandtully, Perthshire, PH9 0PG
Telephone: 01887 447000
Website: www.ballintaggart.com and www.shop.ballintaggart.com
Email: hello@ballintaggart.com
Facebook: Ballintaggart16
Instagram @ballintaggart on
A destination for food lovers in Highland Perthshire. Established in 2016.

BARLEY BREE RESTAURANT WITH ROOMS

6 Willoughby Street, Muthill, PH5 2AB
Telephone: 01764 681451
Website: www.barleybree.com
Email: info@barleybree.com
Facebook: Barley Bree, restaurant with rooms
Twitter and Instagram @barleybree6
Family-run, award-winning restaurant with rooms, nestled in the heart of Muthill, serving French food with the finest Scottish ingredients.

CHARLOTTE FLOWER CHOCOLATES

The Old Schoolhouse, Acharn PH15 2HS
Telephone: 01887 830307
Website: www.charlotteflowerchocolates.com
Email: info@charlotteflowerchocolates.com
Facebook and Instagram @cocoaflower
Based on the south shore of Loch Tay, we gather local, wild flavours to combine with extraordinary chocolate from around the world, to make unique and delicious chocolates.

DELIVINO WILD KITCHEN

Website: www.delivino.co.uk
Email: wildkitchen@delivino.co.uk
Social Media @delivinowildkitchen
Delivino's custom built wood-fired outdoor wild kitchen for outdoor event catering in Perthshire.

DEWAR'S ABERFELDY DISTILLERY

Dewar's Aberfeldy Distillery, Aberfeldy, Perthshire, PH15 2EB
Telephone: 01887 822010
Website: www.dewarsaberfeldydistillery.com
Email: aberfeldydistillery@dewars.com
Instagram and Twitter @DewarsAberfeldy
Facebook: DewarsAbereldyDistillery
Distillery tours take place throughout the day and include our atmospheric warehouse and heritage centre. Whisky bar, shop and café.

GIRAFFE TRADING C.I.C

51-53 South Street, Perth, PH2 8PD
Telephone: 01738 449227
Website: www.giraffe-trading.co.uk
Email: info@giraffe-trading.uk
Facebook: GiraffePerth
LinkedIn: Giraffe-Trading
Instagram and Twitter @giraffeinperth
Perth's first community interest company offering work experience, training and life skills to local people with disadvantages in the workplace.

GLEN LYON COFFEE ROASTERS

Aberfeldy Business Park, Aberfeldy, PH15 2AQ
Telephone: 01887 822871
Website: www.glenlyoncoffee.co.uk
Email: info@glenlyoncoffee.co.uk
Social Media @glenlyoncoffee
Proud to be B Corp Certified, Glen Lyon source and roast some of the world's finest coffee from their base in Aberfeldy.

THE GLENTURRET

The Hosh, Crieff, Perthshire, PH7 4HA
Telephone: 01764 656565
Website: www.theglenturretrestaurant.com
Email: enquiries@theglenturret.com
Facebook and Instagram @theglenturretlalique
LinkedIn: The Glenturret Lalique Restaurant
Daily distillery tours, whisky flights at The Lalique Bar, a dedicated retail store and The Glenturret Lalique Restaurant, the distillery's unique Michelin-starred dining experience.

HIGHLAND BOUNDARY

Kirklandbank Farm, Alyth, PH11 8LL
Website: www.highlandboundary.com
Email: hello@highlandboundary.com
Highland Boundary captures the unique essence of Scotland's wild plants, distilling them into wild-inspired natural spirits and liqueurs with new and remarkable flavours.

IAIN BURNETT HIGHLAND CHOCOLATIER

Grandtully, between Aberfeldy & Pitlochry PH9 0PL
Telephone: 01887 840775
Website: www.HighlandChocolatier.com
Email: iainburnett@highlandchocolatier.com
Twitter @HighlandChoc
Instagram @IainBurnettChocolatier
Facebook: IainBurnettTheHighlandChocolatier
Internationally acclaimed award-winning gourmet chocolates of fresh Scottish cream and rare island cocoa by a Master Chocolatier.

LOCH LEVEN'S LARDER

Channel Farm, Kinross, KY13 9HD
Telephone: 01592 841000
Website: www.lochlevenslarder.com
Email: customerservice@lochlevenslarder.com
Twitter @LochLevenLarder
Instagram @loch_levens_larder
Facebook: Loch Leven's Larder
We're all about sharing delicious food, quality and quirkiness. Spectacular views, food hall, quality gifts and the great outdoors. Open 9-5, 7 days.

MOOR OF RANNOCH RESTAURANT & ROOMS

Rannoch Station, PH17 2QA
Telephone: 01882 633238
Website: www.moorofrannoch.co.uk
Email: info@moorofrannoch.co.uk
Facebook and Twitter @moorofrannoch
Instagram @moor_of_rannoch
Situated beside Rannoch Station, we're a warm, cosy haven offering a chance to retreat, relax, unwind and escape.

MURRAYSHALL COUNTRY ESTATE

Murrayshall Country Estate, Scone PH2 7PH
Telephone: 01738 551171
Website: www.murrayshall.co.uk
Email: info@murrayshall.co.uk
Facebook: Murrayshall Estate
Twitter @Murrayshall
Instagram @murrayshallcountryestate
Luxury, boutique hotel set in 365 acres of countryside, with 40 guest bedrooms and suites, two restaurants, a bar and 27-holes of golf.

THE NORTH PORT

8 North Port, Perth, PH1 5LU
Telephone: 01738 580867
Website: www.thenorthport.co.uk
Friendly restaurant showcasing carefully selected ingredients supplied by local breeders, growers and foragers to create refined, inventive dishes.

PERTH FARMERS' MARKET

20 Bleachers Way, Huntingtowerfield, Perth, PH1 3NY
Telephone: 01738 582159 / 07732 483729
Website: www.perthfarmersmarket.co.uk
Facebook: PerthFarmersMkt
Twitter @Perthfarmersmkt
A monthly outdoor market offering an array of quality local produce in the heart of the city.

THE PICKLED PEACOCK

East Inchmichael Farm, PH2 7SP
Telephone: 01821 642163
Website: www.pickled-peacock.co.uk
Email: hello@speakscotland.co.uk
Instagram @thepickledpeacock
Facebook: PickledP
The Pickled Peacock is a unique, quirky and memorable destination for all the family to enjoy, where musicians, artists and foodies are celebrated alike.

REDWOOD WINES

12 Bridge Street, Dunkeld, PH8 0AH
Telephone: 01350 729228
Website: www.redwoodwines.co.uk
Email: contact@redwoodwines.co.uk
Instagram @redwoodwines
A sophisticated and friendly neighbourhood wine shop & bar in the idyllic village of Dunkeld. Handcrafted charcuterie alongside delectable small plates that perfectly pair with the wine.

RESTAURANT ANDREW FAIRLIE

The Gleneagles Hotel, Auchterarder PH3 1NF
Telephone: 01764 694267
Website: www.andrewfairlie.co.uk
Email: reservations@andrewfairlie.co.uk
Facebook: Andrew Fairlie 2 Michelin Star
Instagram @restaurant_andrew_fairlie
Intimate gastronomic restaurant found at the heart of the iconic Gleneagles Hotel.

SUMMER HARVEST

Ferneyfold Farm, Madderty, Crieff PH7 3PE
Telephone: 01764 683288
Website: www.summerharvestoils.co.uk
Email: info@summerharvestoils.cp.uk
Facebook: SummerHarvestOils
Twitter @summer_harvest
Instagram @summerharvest
Cold Pressed Rapeseed Oil grown, pressed and bottled on the family farm in Perthshire.

TABLA

Address: 173 South Street, Perth, PH2 8NY
Telephone: 01738 444630
Website: www.tablarestaurant.co.uk
Instagram @tablaindianrestaurant
Authentic Indian dining experiences combining the best produce from around the UK with spices grown on the owners' family farms in India to create delicious dishes for the restaurant, takeaway, cook school and Curry Club.

THE TAYBANK

Address: The Taybank, Tay Terrace, Dunkeld, Perthshire, PH80AQ
Website: www.thetaybank.co.uk
Email: info@thetaybank.co.uk
Facebook, Instagram and Twitter @thetaybank
Bar, restaurant, rooms and gardens in the heart of historic Dunkeld.

TAYMOUTH COURTYARD SHOP

Mains of Taymouth, Kenmore PH152HN
Telephone: 01887 830756
Website: www.taymouthcourtyard.com
Email: info@taymouthcourtyard.com
Facebook: taymouthcourtyardshop
Twitter @courtyardshop
Instagram @taymouth_courtyard_shop
The Courtyard Shop offers its customers the very best Scottish food and drink available in the area, and also boasts a selection of books, gifts and clothing for all ages.

THYME DELI & BISTRO AT ERRICHEL

Address: Errichel, Crieff Road, Aberfeldy, Perthshire, PH15 2EL
Telephone: 01887 820850
Website: www.errichel.co.uk
Email: hello@Errichel.co.uk
Facebook: Errichel and Thyme To Eat Scotland
Instagram @errichel and @thymedelibistro
Where field meets fork: Thyme Deli & Bistro at Errichel is a working hill-farm and foodie destination, offering dining, shopping and farm stays above picturesque Aberfeldy in Highland Perthshire.

WILD HEARTH BAKERY

Address: 15A Cultybraggan Camp, Comrie, PH6 2AB
Telephone: 07909 295596
Website: www.WildHearthBakery.com
Email: john@wildhearthbakery.com
Facebook and Instagram @wildhearthbakery
Wood-fired artisan sourdough bakery on the edge of the Scottish Highlands.

THE PERTHSHIRE COOK BOOK

First edition printed in 2022 in the UK

ISBN: 978-1-915538-03-1

Compiled by: Chris Rowley & Sarah Russell

Written by: Katie Fisher

Photography by: Clair Irwin

Designed by: Phil Turner & Paul Cocker

Sales & PR: Emma Toogood & Lizzy Capps

Contributors: Lis Ellis, Joe Food & Lizzie Morton

me:ze
PUBLISHING

Published by Meze Publishing Limited
Unit 1b, 2 Kelham Square
Kelham Riverside
Sheffield S3 8SD
Web: www.mezepublishing.co.uk
Telephone: 0114 275 7709
Email: info@mezepublishing.co.uk

Printed in Great Britain by Bell and Bain Ltd, Glasgow